Get on Track to FCE

Language Practice Workbook

Contents

Mary Stephens

1 One world

Speaking ▶ CB p.7

1 Giving personal information

▶▶ *speaking strategy*

When you answer questions about yourself, try to answer in full. Don't just give one-word answers. ◀◀

1 Put the words into the correct order to make sentences.

1 to and go I'd law like study to university
I'd like to go to university and study law.

2 brothers have I older sister three and one

....

3 a block of flats centre I in near live the town

....

4 to do because I so much love my there is town

....

5 with I my a older room share sister

....

6 Saturdays friends I in often meet my town on

....

7 so I can live I every morning my near school there walk

....

8 free I in like listening music my time to.

....

2 Match the questions with each of the sentences above.

a) How do you get to school every day? ...7...
b) Have you got your own bedroom or do you share? ....
c) What hobbies have you got? ....
d) What do you want to do when you leave school? ....
e) Do you live in a house or a flat? ....
f) What do you usually do at the weekend? ....
g) How many brothers and sisters have you got? ....
h) Do you like living in your town? ....

3 Now write your own answers to each of the questions above in your notebook.

2 so and neither / nor

grammar file

so / neither / nor + auxiliary + pronoun

1 A: *I'm enjoying* this video. B: *So am I.*
2 A: *I love* football. B: *So do I / So does* my brother.
3 A: *Anna had* a shock. B: *So did we.*
4 A: *I don't speak* German. B: *Nor / Neither do I.*
5 A: *I didn't go* to the party. B: *Nor / Neither did we.*

1 Match a statement in Column A with an appropriate reply in Column B.

A	B
1 I love rock music.	a) Nor do I.
2 I can't speak French.	b) Neither is ours.
3 My dad owns his own business.	c) So am I.
4 Our flat isn't very big.	d) So do I.
5 I've got two brothers and sisters.	e) Nor can I.
6 My best friend doesn't live in my street.	f) Neither does mine.
7 I don't like tidying my room.	g) So does mine.
8 I'm studying very hard at the moment.	h) So have I.

2 Now write the correct reply to each of A's statements below, using *neither / nor* or *so* and the subject in brackets.

1 A: I like listening to music. (I)
   B: *So do I.*

2 A: My brother can't drive. (mine)
   B: Nor ....

3 A: I can play the guitar quite well. (I)
   B: So ....

4 A: My mum doesn't work full-time. (my mum)
   B: ....

5 A: We haven't got any pets. (we)
   B: ....

6 A: My sister goes to the same school as me. (mine)
   B: ....

Reading ▶ CB pp.8–9

1 Definitions

Replace the words in *italics* with an appropriate word from the list.

context / skills / official / strategies / native speakers / cultural awareness / multi-lingual environment / last but not least

1 The number of people who speak English as a second language is now greater than the number of *people who speak it as their first language.* ..*native speakers*....

2 English is now an *approved* second language in over 70 countries. ....

3 People are increasingly likely to work in a *situation where people speak many languages.* ....
....

4 When you learn a language, *knowing about the culture* is just as important as language skills. ....
....

5 There are certain *methods* you can use to develop your reading, writing and listening skills. ....
....

6 When you translate, you are not developing your foreign language *abilities.* ....

7 When you are reading, try to guess the meaning of unknown words from the *situation.* ....
....

8 *Finally,* keep a vocabulary notebook. ....
....

2 Guessing meaning from context

▶▶ *reading strategy*

If you come across a new word, try to use the context to help you work out the meaning. ◀◀

1 Read the short text below and try to work out the meaning of the words in *italics*.

Conchita was walking through the rainforest when she was attacked by a (1) *jeeboa*. It had climbed one of the tall (2) *ciradas* which grow in the forest and leapt down on her as she walked beneath it. Although it was twice her size, she was able to fight it off using a sharp (3) *carbosh* which she always carried with her for protection. Fortunately, she was not badly hurt but her body was black and blue with (4) *pointads*.

2 Now <u>underline</u> the correct option.

1 A jeeboa is a type of *tree / animal.*

2 A cirada is a type of *animal / tree* .

3 A carbosh is a type of *knife / bag.*

4 A pointad is a sort of *clothing / injury.*

3 Ways of recording vocabulary

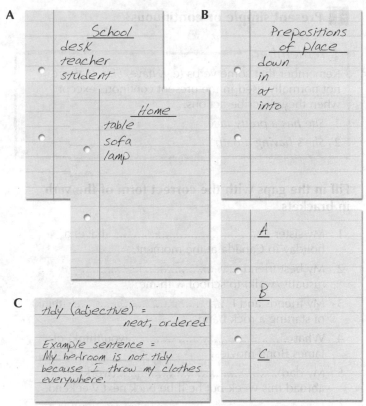

A
School
desk
teacher
student

Home
table
sofa
lamp

B
Prepositions
of place
down
in
at
into

A
B
C

C
tidy (adjective) =
neat, ordered

Example sentence =
My bedroom is not tidy
because I throw my clothes
everywhere.

Match each picture with one method of recording vocabulary.

1 Write new words on individual cards. ....

2 List words in alphabetical order. ....

3 Put words on different pages, according to the topic. ....

4 Organise words by grammatical category. ....

4 Prepositions

Fill in the gaps with the correct preposition from the list. You may need to use a word more than once.

down / in / at / into

1 More people speak Chinese now than ..*at*... any time ..*in*... the past.

2 French is the second language .... a number of countries.

3 When you're learning a foreign language, it's not a good idea to translate everything .... your own language.

4 You should try hard to speak English all the time when you're .... an English class.

5 Try to guess the meaning of a word before you look it up .... a dictionary.

6 It's a good idea to write .... new words and phrases in a special vocabulary book.

Grammar ▶ CB p.10, grammar file 4

1 Present simple or continuous?

> ! *remember*
>
> Remember that some verbs (e.g. *have, like, feel*) are
> not normally used in the present continous except
> when they describe actions.
> 1 She **has** a pretty face.
> 2 She**'s having** a bath.

**Fill in the gaps with the correct form of the verb
in brackets.**

1 My sister .... (have) a
   holiday in Canada at the moment.
2 My best friend ....
   (usually/walk) to school with me.
3 My friends and I .... (think)
   of starting a rock band.
4 What .... (you/think) of
   James Bond movies?
5 My dad .... (work)
   abroad this week but he'll be back next weekend.
6 I .... (take) my dog for a
   walk nearly every night.
7 You .... (look) worried.
   What's the mattter?
8 I .... (look) for my wallet.
   Have you seen it?
9 I .... (not/go out)
   during the week; I ....
   (usually/stay) at home.
10 .... (this book/belong)
   to you?

2 Questions

**Your friend is on holiday in Great Britain. You
decide to send her an e-mail asking her about
the holiday. Use the prompts to make questions.**

1 you/have/good time/in Britain?
   Are you having a good time in Britain?
2 Which hotel/you/stay at?
   ....
3 you/like/the way of life/over there?
   ....

4 What special things/you/want/to see/while you
   are there?
   ....
5 English people/speak/very quickly?
   ....
6 the sun/shine/at the moment or/it/rain?
   ....
7 What time/people/normally/have dinner/over there?
   ....
8 you/go sightseeing/every day?
   ....

3 Frequency adverbs

**Rewrite these sentences in your notebook, putting
the adverbs in brackets in the correct position.**

1 We watch TV in the evenings. (rarely)
   We rarely watch TV in the evenings.
2 My brother and I don't fight. (often)
3 I go shopping in the town centre.
   (sometimes/at weekends)
4 Do you go out with your friends?
   (usually/in the evenings)
5 My mum drives my sister and me to the beach.
   (now and again)
6 I tidy my bedroom. (never/in the morning)
7 I stay at school after classes have finished. (seldom)
8 My best friend comes round to my house.
   (once or twice a week)

4 Find the mistake

**One sentence is correct. Tick it. <u>Underline</u> the
mistakes in the other sentences and correct them.**

1 I <u>am not agree</u> with what you said. ......*don't agree*......
2 My cousin work in the local hospital. ....
3 I stay always at my friend's house on Fridays.
   ....
4 Does your mother usually goes out to work?
   ....
5 One of my friends is living in the USA in the moment.
   ....
6 My sister and I don't go often out together.
   ....
7 My brother John doesn't actually lives at home now.
   ....
8 Do you understand what that man is saying?
   ....

5 Extra word

There is one unnecessary word in each sentence below. Cross it out.

1 How many people ~~they~~ live in your flat?

2 I meet usually my friends once or twice a week.

3 My boyfriend lives in the same part of town as me I do.

4 My favourite hobby it is playing the guitar.

5 My dad is a doctor and mum does works in a hotel.

6 I love music so I'm learning now to play the flute.

7 On the Saturdays, I normally meet my friends in town.

8 Do you and your family go usually on holiday together?

Vocabulary ▶ CB p.11

Using an English–English dictionary

Look at the list of abbreviations and grammar codes. Then look at the dictionary extracts and answer the questions.

1 Is *leaves* the plural of *leaf*? Circle the correct answer.

   Yes / No

2 Is *leisure* a countable or uncountable noun?

   It's ....

3 Write down the past simple and past participle of the verb *leave*.

   ....

4 What sort of verb is *leave off*? Is it formal or informal?

   It's a .... verb.

   It's ....

5 Find the word *lecture* in the extract. Do you *make* or *give* a lecture?

   You .... a lecture.

6 Find *legal* in the extract. What is the opposite?

   ....

7 Study the pictures. Which of the words in *italics* is correct?

   'I *lent / borrowed* my friend some money.'

   ....

8 Look at the entries for *left* and complete this sentence:

   '*My room is the second door* ....
   the left.'

Abbreviations

adj = adjective
adv = adverb
n = noun
phr v = phrasal verb
v = verb

Grammar codes

[C] = Countable
[U] = Uncountable
[singular] shows that a noun is always singular and must be followed by a singular noun.
[T] = Transitive. Transitive verbs must have an object.
[I] = Intransitive. Intransitive verbs do not have an object.
[I,T] = Transitive or Intransitive
[only before noun] shows that an adjective is always used before a noun

---

leaf[1] /liːf/ *n* [C], *plural* **leaves** /liːvz/ **1** one of the flat green parts of a plant that are joined to its stem or branches **2 take a leaf out of someone's book** to behave like someone else because you admire them **3 turn over a new leaf** to start to behave in a much better way

leave[1] /liːv/ *v* left /left/, left, leaving **1** [I,T] to go away from a place or person: *What time did you leave the office?* | *She left him watching the television.* **2** [I,T] to stop doing a job, going to a school, or being a member of an organization: *She left her job in order to have a baby.* **3** [I,T] to stop living somewhere and move to another place: *Nick doesn't want to leave California.* **4** [I,T] to end your relationship with your husband, a girlfriend etc: *His wife left him and he started drinking heavily.* | **+ for** *We're leaving for Paris tomorrow.* **5** [T] to put something somewhere: *Just leave those letters on my desk, please.* **6** [T] to let something stay in a particular state or condition: *Can we leave the dishes for later?* **7** [T] if you leave food or drink, you do not eat or drink all of it, often because you do not like it **8** [T] also **leave behind** to forget to take something with you when you leave a place: **leave sth on/at etc** *Oh no, I think I've left my keys in the front door.* **9 be left (over)** to remain after everything else has been taken away or used: *Is there any coffee left?* **10 leave sb alone** to stop annoying or upsetting someone: *Just go away and leave me alone.* **11 leave sth alone** spoken to stop touching something: *Leave that watch alone – you'll break it!* **12 leave sth to sb** to let someone decide something or be responsible for something: *I've always left financial decisions to my wife.* **13** [T] to give something to someone after you die: **leave sb sth** *My aunt left me this ring.*
leave sth behind *phr v* [T] to forget to take something with you when you leave a place
leave off *phr v* [I,T] *informal* to stop doing something: *Let's start from where we left off yesterday.*
leave sb/sth ↔ out *phr v* [T] to not include someone or something in a group, list, or activity: *She was upset about being left out of the team.*

lec·ture[1] /ˈlektʃələr/ *n* [C] **1** a talk to a group of people about a subject: **+ on** *a lecture on Islamic art* | **give a lecture** *Dr. Hill gave a brilliant lecture.* **2** a long serious talk that criticizes someone or warns them about something: **+ on/ about** *I'm sick of Dad's lectures about my clothes.*

le·gal /ˈliːgəl/ *adj* **1** allowed or done according to the law: *a legal agreement* →opposite ILLEGAL **2** relating to the law: *the legal system* | **take legal action** (=when you ask a court to punish someone or force someone to do something) —**legally** *adv* —**legality** /lɪˈgæləti/ *n* [U]

Mark lent Julie £10. Julie borrowed £10 from Mark.

Julie paid Mark back the following week.

left[1] /left/ *adj* [only before noun] **1** on the side of your body that contains your heart: *Jim's broken his left leg.* **2** in the direction that is opposite to the right: *Take a left turn at the lights.*

left[2] *adv* towards the left side: *Turn left at the church.* → opposite RIGHT[2]

left[3] *n* **1** [singular] the left side or direction: **on the/your left** *It's the second door on your left.* **2 the Left** political parties or groups that believe that wealth should be shared out more equally, for example Socialists → opposite RIGHT[3]

lei·sure /ˈleʒəˈliːzər/ *n* **1** [U] time when you are not working and can do things you enjoy: *leisure activities such as sailing and swimming* **2 at your leisure** as slowly as you want or when you want: *Read it at your leisure.*

Writing: expanding notes

▶ CB pp.13–14

1 Expanding notes into sentences

Turn these notes into sentences, starting with the word given.

1 live in small village / parents and younger sister

    I *live in a small village with my parents and my younger sister* .

2 share room with sister = OK because good friends

    I ....

    but ....

3 free time = go cinema, meet friends in park

    In my ....

    ....

4 best friend = girl called Sarah, lives block of flats in next street to mine

    My ....

    who ....

5 want to be doctor and work in Africa

    I ....

    ....

6 fav. band = Hearsay but prefer solo singers, e.g. Robbie Williams.

    My ....

    ....

3 Writing task

Read this e-mail which has been sent to you by a student in the USA. Then write your reply in 120–180 words. You should write three main paragraphs in your letter.

> Well, enough about me. It's your turn now! Please write and tell me something about yourself, your everyday life and the part of the country you live in.

2 Correct a sample answer

Read the writing task on p.14 of your Coursebook and look at this sample answer. The student has not paragraphed the letter correctly and has sometimes forgotten to expand notes into complete sentences. Write the letter in your notebook in three paragraphs, correcting any mistakes.

▶▶ *writing strategy*

Always check your work for basic errors. You can do this while you are writing. Make sure you check the whole text through again very carefully after you have finished. ◀◀

Dear Barbara,
Thanks for your letter – I really enjoyed reading it. It was really interesting to hear about you∟ your family. ∟about myself. There are six people in my family: mum, dad and four children. Dad's∟ businessman. He travels abroad a lot. ∟works very long hours. Mum's a dentist. I've got three brothers – ∟older than me and are at university in another part of the country. They just come home during∟ holidays. I love living here in London. It's great and∟ always something to do. We live in∟ suburbs but it's easy to get to the centre by train. I often go there shopping with my friends or to a concert in the evenings. My favourite hobby is dancing – I would love to be∟ professional dancer when I leave school. I go∟ special classes. Sometimes I even win prizes! Well, must stop now – I've got lots of homework to do.
Write back soon!
Yours,
Maria

Remember to:

• brainstorm your ideas. Think of the three main topics you have to write about and make notes in your notebook under each heading.

Myself

My everyday life

The part of the country I live in

• write a separate paragraph for each of the topics.

• edit your work when you have finished.

2 Sport

Speaking ▶ CB p.15

1 Word sets: sports

__Underline__ the odd word out in each set.

1 helmet, <u>paddle</u>, gloves, boots
2 court, track, pole, pitch
3 team, player, spectator, boxing
4 exciting, popular, stamina, interesting
5 net, helmet, trainers, swimming cap
6 ball, agile, board, bat

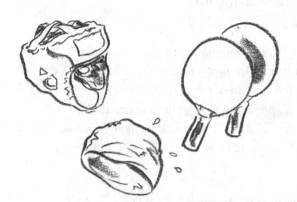

2 Comparing and contrasting photos

> ▶▶ *speaking strategy*
>
> When you are comparing two photos, remember to identify clearly which one you are talking about. ◀◀

1 Read the text, which compares and contrasts the sports in the photos. Then choose the best option A or B to fill in the gaps.

The people in (1) .... *both* .... of these photos are (2) .... different kinds of sport. In the first photo, the men are playing rugby. In the second photo, the woman is doing something like flying. I'm not sure what it's called but I think it's hang-gliding.

Rugby is a (3) .... game but you can (4) .... hang-gliding by yourself, I suppose. <u>I don't think</u> (5) .... of the sports are very safe – they look quite dangerous to me. The hang-glider is wearing a (6) ...., while the rugby players are dressed in T-shirts and (7) .... I suppose rugby is quite a rough, noisy (8) .... but hang-gliding looks very peaceful. I think you need to be fit to do both sports. I'd prefer to go hang-gliding because I imagine it's more exciting.

1	A	all	B	both
2	A	making	B	doing
3	A	team	B	crowd
4	A	go	B	get
5	A	neither	B	either
6	A	cap	B	helmet
7	A	shorts	B	tracksuits
8	A	play	B	game

2 <u>Underline</u> the words or phrases the speaker uses to:

a) give an opinion   c) state a preference

b) refer to each of the photos   d) contrast two statements

Reading ▶ CB pp.16–17

1 Verbs

Fill in the gaps with a verb from the list.

become / do / have / join / pass / wear

1 Fiona decided to .... the national team when she was 12.
2 She has to .... a helmet for protection.
3 She has just .... the captain of her team.
4 Her team often .... problems finding time to practise.
5 In ice hockey, you have to .... the puck to another player.
6 Fiona managed to .... a lot of training exercises in the gym last week.

2 Prepositions/Prepositional phrases

Fill in the gaps with a suitable preposition from the list.

at / over / for / at / to / in / of

1 Fiona started ice-hockey lessons .... the age .... 10.
2 She can skate .... 40 kilometres an hour.
3 She can play alongside anyone .... the squad.
4 She has to wear a helmet with a cage .... her face.
5 When people meet Fiona face .... face, they are surprised to hear she is an ice-hockey player.
6 Fiona is responsible .... her own fitness programme.

3 Definitions

Replace the words in *italics* with an appropriate word from the list.

discouraged / come together / bruises / fit / sessions / face to face / joined / tough

1 Ice hockey is a *difficult and challenging* sport. ....
2 Kathryn *became a member of* the national team at the age of 16. ....
3 She wears protective clothing but she still gets lots of *marks on her skin*. ....
4 Ice hockey is fast so players must be *in good condition*. ....
5 Kathryn had quite a few *periods of time* in the gym last week. ....
6 People are surprised when they meet Kathryn *in person* because she isn't very tall. ....
7 The whole squad *meet* for week-long training camps from time to time. ....
8 Ice hockey is not an easy sport, but Kathryn never feels *she lacks the confidence to continue*. ....

Grammar ▶ CB p.18,

grammar files 5, 6

1 Past simple or present perfect simple?

Fill in the gaps with the correct form of the verb in brackets.

A: (1) .... (you/see) the football match on TV yesterday?
B: No. Who (2) .... (win)?
A: Germany of course! They (3) .... (be) the best team around for a while now.
B: Yes, they (4) .... (win) three major championships now, haven't they? Was it a good match?
A: Yes, both teams (5) .... (play) really well.
...
B: You (6) .... (have) a game of table tennis yesterday, didn't you? How long did the match last?
A: Oh, it (7) .... (go on) for hours. We (8) .... (be) exhausted at the end!
B: I'm not surprised. I (9) .... (never/play) table tennis in my life.
A: Really? Well, my friends and I (10) .... (just/book) the hall for a return match. Why don't you play too?
B: Great! What time?

2 Time expressions

<u>Underline</u> the correct word in each pair.

1 I have *ever/<u>never</u>* been on a sailing holiday.
2 Have you finished with these tennis racquets *yet/already*?
3 Those boys have been playing baseball *for/since* 2 o'clock.
4 My brother *still/yet* hasn't learnt how to swim properly.
5 Haven't you *never/ever* been to a football match?
6 We waited outside the football stadium *for/since* ages.
7 Venus Williams has *already/yet* won two Wimbledon Championships.
8 Barcelona has *still/just* scored the winning goal!

3 Present perfect simple or continuous?

Fill in the gaps with the correct form of the verb in brackets.

A: Hello, Roger. Congratulations on winning the windsurfing competition! Tell me, how long (1) .... (be) interested in this sport?

B: Six years. I (2) .... (windsurf) since I was 12.

A: And how many competitions (3) .... (you/win) so far?

B: This is the first, so I'm on top of the world! ...

A: Your father is a keen windsurfer. (4) .... (he/be able to) help you train for this event?

B: Well, he can't windsurf just now because he (5) .... (break) his arm. But that (6) .... (never/stop) him coming to watch! He's got lots of free time now because he (7) .... (just/retire) from his job. ...

A: You (8) .... (prepare) for the competition for the past year. (9) .... (you/have) any free time for hobbies?

B: Yes. One of my hobbies is reading. I (10) .... (read) about three novels this month! I (11) .... (also/start) diving lessons. Life (12) .... (be) really busy just recently!

4 Past simple, present perfect or present perfect continuous?

There is a tense mistake in each of these sentences. Underline it and write the sentences correctly in your notebook.

1 My hair is wet because I <u>have swum</u>.
 My hair is wet because I have been swimming.
2 Have you heard the news? Our team has just been winning the Cup!
3 My team has scored three goals but the other side still won the game!
4 We have had hockey practice after school yesterday.
5 We waited to play tennis since 3 o'clock but it's still raining.
6 My brother has been playing baseball really well when he was at school.
7 Ella won three tournaments so far this year.
8 Our Olympic athletes trained for months and they haven't finished yet.

5 Rewriting

Complete the second sentence so that it means the same as the first.

1 I'm watching a rugby match for the first time.
 I *have never watched* .... a rugby match before.
2 Jack began to play football a year ago. He's still playing.
 Jack .... football for a year.
3 The football team started training. They stopped two hours later.
 The football team .... for two hours.
4 I know Georgia. I met her six years ago.
 I .... Georgia for six years.
5 I started having riding lessons ages ago. I still have them.
 I .... riding lessons for ages.
6 The last time I saw Sampras play tennis was two years ago.
 I .... Sampras play tennis for two years.
7 I got this watch six years ago. I still have it.
 I .... this watch for six years.
8 Jason went to Canada in 2001. He returned home in 2002.
 He .... in Canada for a year.

Vocabulary ▶ CB p.19

Word sets: action verbs

boxing / squash / football / hockey / tennis / baseball

In which of the sports listed do you:

1 **hit the ball** with a bat? ....

2 **score a goal** by kicking the ball into the net? ....

3 **punch someone** while wearing large gloves? ....

4 **tackle another person** with your stick? ....

5 **serve and volley a ball** across a net? ....

6 **hit a ball** against a wall with a racquet? ....

What's the word?

Fill in the gaps with an appropriate word.

1 The person who controls a football match is called a ....

2 There are 11 players in a football ....

3 In games like tennis or squash, the person you play against is called your ....

4 In most games, if you score more points than the other player, you .... the game.

5 Most ice-hockey players .... helmets and other protective clothes.

6 When you play a competitive game you want to .... the other team.

7 Most sports people would like to .... a gold medal in the Olympics.

8 To .... a goal in hockey, you have to get the ball into the net.

3 Prepositions

Fill in the gaps with one of the words from the list. Do not use the same word twice.

against / off / with / over / into / in / to / between

1 Beckham passed the ball .... another member of the team.

2 Jackson caught the ball .... his right hand.

3 The baseball player hit the ball .... his bat.

4 Munich were playing .... a local team.

5 In football, you score by kicking the ball .... the posts and .... the net.

6 The referee held up a red card and sent the player .... the football field.

7 The ice-hockey player wore a helmet with a cage right .... her face.

4 Open cloze

Read the text and decide which word from the list best fits each space. Use only one word in each space.

at / from / is / of / to / went / with / of

MIRACLE SWIMMER

Champion swimmer Celine Williams used to be really scared (1) .... water. She never (2) .... swimming with the other kids. She wouldn't even go (3) .... the beach. That all changed the day she met sports psychologist Andy Taylor. Andy taught her to face her fears instead of running away (4) .... them. Three years on, she is delighted (5) .... the results. 'It's a miracle,' she told reporters. 'I only started swimming lessons a year ago. I thought I would be useless (6) .... it. Now I'm a medal winner!' As you can imagine, Andy (7) .... pleased with Celine's achievement. 'It's taken a lot of courage,' he said, 'and I'm really proud (8) .... her.'

Writing: topic sentences ▶ CB pp.21–22

1 Planning

A student has been asked to write a letter about a recent visit to her grandparents.

1 Read the notes she made.

1 they have great sense of humour + they really know how to enjoy life
2 have been having wonderful time
3 have met lots of people in village and made lots of new friends
4 not as busy as my town – but still plenty to do
5 my grandparents = best in world!
6 on last day, went for picnic with them
7 my grandparents' village = about 80 km away
8 they're not strict or old-fashioned
9 they've lived there all their lives (+ they know everybody)

2 Match the notes with the correct heading.

   A
   My grandparents
   …   …   …

   B
   The place where they live
   …   …   …

   C
   What I've been doing
   …   …   …

3 Expand the notes into sentences.

4 Now tick which sentence under each heading would make the best topic sentence.

▶▶ *writing strategy*
Make sure you have a topic sentence in each paragraph which summarises the content. That will make your letter easier to follow.
◀◀

5 Put the sentences in the best order.

2 Correct a sample answer

Read the writing task on p.22 of your Coursebook and look at this sample answer. Unfortunately, the student has not paragraphed the letter. First, <u>underline</u> the topic sentences in the text. Then mark where each new paragraph should begin with a line (/).

Dear James,
I've just received your letter. Sorry I didn't write before but I've been so busy during the last few weeks. To start with, my teacher has chosen me to play in the school volleyball team! I can't believe it and I'm very excited! I've got to practise every night so I've been staying at school really late recently. The big match is next Saturday. All my family and friends are coming to watch – I just hope we win! The other thing is that I've got a new girlfriend. She goes to my school. I've known her for ages but not very well. Her name's Gloria and she's 15 years old. Anyway, we meet every weekend – we usually go to the cinema or a disco or something. As for my holidays, well I haven't made any plans yet. Maybe we'll go to the beach like last year. I'd like to visit you in America but it's too expensive. Must go now – I'm a very busy man!
All the best,
    Steve

3 Writing task

You have just come back from a visit to your grandparents in another town. Write a letter to an English-speaking friend, telling him/her about your grandparents, where they live and what you have been doing. Write about 120–180 words in your notebook.

Remember to:

• plan your work before you begin.

3 Friends and family

Speaking ► CB p.23

Prioritising and giving opinions

▶▶ *speaking strategy*

When you are having a discussion, give your opinions clearly but make sure you ask your partner for his/her opinions too. Don't be aggressive, or try to dominate the discussion too much. ◀◀

Look at the phrases in the box which you can use when asking for and giving an opinion and for agreeing. Then fill in the gaps in the dialogue with a suitable phrase.

> What do you think?   I agree (with you/him/her).
> Yes, you're right.   But I also think that …
> I imagine/suppose …
> For me, .. / In my opinion, the most important thing is …
> … is/are important for me.
> Which is/are the most important for you?
> The most important for me is/are … because …

A: Which two personal characteristics do (1) .... are most important in a husband or wife?

B: I (2) .... a sense of humour is important. What (3) ...., Carlos?

A: For me, the most (4) .... loyalty, because without it you have no marriage really.

B: Yes, I (5) .... Well, (6) .... do you .... the second most important characteristic is?

A: In my (7) ...., it's patience. I (8) .... you need a lot of that when you're married.

B: Yes, you're (9) ....! But I (10) .... that unselfishness is important, too.

A: Yes, that's true.

Reading ► CB pp.24–25

1 Reference links

The following sentences summarise the story on pp.24–25 of your Coursebook, but they are in the wrong order.

1 Fill in the gaps with a preposition from the list. The verb is in *italics* to help you. Do not worry about the order yet.

around / on / out of / above / over / with / to / up / over / up / on

- ☐ a) On his way back, Jon *stumbled* ..*over*... Liz's bag and *spilled* the coffee all ..*over*... her coat.
- ☐ b) Some time later, Liz *got* .... the train and took the seat opposite him.
- ☑ c) One Friday, Jon missed his train and had to *hang* .... at the station.
- ☐ d) There was a rack .... the seat.
- ☐ e) It left a stain – and Jon went red .... embarrassment.
- ☐ f) Liz apologised for this, but Jon didn't even *look* ....; he just *stared* .... the window.
- ☐ g) A little while after this incident, Jon *went* .... the dining car to get some coffee.
- ☐ h) Liz *got* .... to put her bag there – and *stepped* .... Jon's foot.

2 Then number the sentences in the correct order. Underline the reference links that helped you decide.

2 Words that go together

Fill in the gaps with a verb from the list. The noun is in *italics* to help you.

book / join / make / miss / spill / watch

1 If you .... a *promise*, I expect you to keep it!
2 We didn't have tickets for the play so we just had to .... *the queue*.
3 Why don't we stay in tonight and .... *a film*?
4 My friend pushed me and made me .... *my drink*.
5 I think I'll .... *a ticket* for the rock concert.
6 Come on! We'll .... *our train* if you don't hurry!

Grammar ▶ CB p.26, grammar file 6

1 Past simple or past continuous?

<u>Underline</u> the correct option in each pair.

1 Amanda *rang / was ringing* her boyfriend every day while he was in Japan.

2 I *went / was going* to bed after the film finished.

3 We *were playing / played* cards while we *waited / were waiting* for the train to arrive.

4 My cousin knew he wanted to marry his future wife as soon as he *met / was meeting* her.

5 I *sat / was sitting* in the park when something unusual happened.

6 I *was swimming / swam* every day while I was on holiday.

7 We met in the town centre and *had / were having* coffee together.

8 My aunt *fell / was falling* as she was getting out of her car and *broke / was breaking* her leg.

9 *Did you make / Were you making* any new friends while you were on holiday?

10 How *did Lisa react / was Lisa reacting* when Richard asked her to marry him?

2 Past perfect (continuous) or past simple?

Fill in the gaps using the verbs in brackets.

1 My friend was really pleased because her boyfriend .... (ring) her earlier.

2 Before meeting the man she married, my sister .... (never go out with) anyone.

3 After my mother .... (be) in Poland for just a month, she .... (meet) my father.

4 By the time Peter .... (get) to the party, his girlfriend .... (already/leave).

5 Tony was hot and sweaty because he .... (play) football all morning.

6 We .... (rush) to the airport, but our cousins' plane .... (still / not / arrive).

7 Laura .... (never / be) a bridesmaid before so she felt nervous about the wedding.

8 In the morning, the roads were dangerous because it .... (snow) all night.

9 When my sister .... (get) home last night, she .... (discover) that she .... (lose) her engagement ring.

10 We .... (already / buy) the couple a wedding present when we .... (hear) that they .... (cancel) the wedding.

3 Find the mistake

There are ten tense mistakes in this text. <u>Underline</u> them and write the text correctly in your notebook.

When Tony and Amy first met, they didn't like each other at all. In fact, they <u>were having</u> a terrible argument.

They were in the disco when it happened. Amy sat with her friends when Tony came up and was asking her to dance. She had refused and went on talking to the girl next to her. The chair on the other side was empty, so Tony had sat down. Unfortunately, Amy was putting her sunglasses on that same chair a short time earlier! When Tony realised what he did he was terribly embarrassed. He was apologising, of course, but Amy was very angry.

The next day, Amy came out of school when she was hearing someone calling her. It was Tony. He was standing there holding a big bunch of flowers and a new pair of sunglasses, which he was buying for her earlier. Amy was really pleased. When Tony asked her to go out with him that night, she accepted immediately!

4 Open cloze

Fill in the gaps with a word from the list.

continued / could / had / have / became /
not / was / were

LOVE ON THE INTERNET!

Lancelot and Vemtira (1) .... friends over the Internet. But they couldn't meet because they lived so far from each other. At that time, Lancelot (2) .... living in Kentucky and Vemtira was in Texas. So they (3) .... to 'chat' on the Net. After a few weeks, they realised they (4) .... falling in love. But they still had (5) .... met!

Then, one day, Lancelot finally made the 800 mile trip. At last he (6) .... see the young woman he (7) .... dreamt about for so long. The minute their eyes met, they knew this was something very real! Lancelot and Vemtira (8) .... been talking about marriage for some time now. It seems it won't be long before the great day is here!

Vocabulary ▶ CB p.27

1 Word sets: relatives

1 Look at the words in the box. Put them under the correct heading. One word can go in both columns.

Male	Female
nephew	

uncle   daughter   ~~nephew~~   stepfather   widow
fiancée   cousin   grandmother   brother-in-law
aunt   widower   son   niece   great-grandfather
bachelor   stepmother

2 Now describe the relationship between the following people using the family tree.

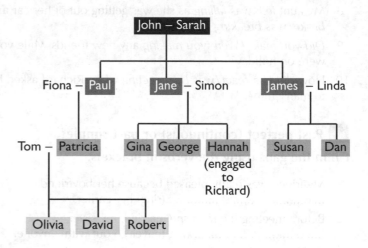

1 Susan and Tom
   Susan is ....*Tom's cousin*.................................. .
2 Simon and Linda
   Simon is ....
3 John and Patricia
   Patricia is ....
4 Hanna and Richard
   Richard is ....
5 Paul and Dan
   Dan is ....
6 Gina and Susan
   Gina is ....
7 Sarah and Robert
   Sarah is ....
8 Olivia and George
   Olivia is ....

Descriptive adjectives

Find the words in the puzzle that mean the opposite of the following words.

S	E	R	I	O	U	S	A	S	
F	A	I	R	N	N	H	O	O	
A	N	G	R	M	A	Y	S	C	
T	S	L	Y	O	P	N	H	I	
I	T	U	V	O	A	E	O	A	
P	U	C	A	D	L	S	R	B	
A	P	K	E	Y	E	F	T	L	
M	I	S	E	R	A	B	L	E	
S	D	E	P	R	E	T	T	Y	

1 tall   *short*
2 dark-haired   ....
3 plain   ....
4 funny   ....
5 tanned   ....
6 cheerful   ....
7 intelligent   ....
8 unfriendly   ....
9 good-tempered   ....
10 self-confident ....

Compound adjectives

1 Match a word in Column A with a word in Column B to make compound nouns.

A	B
1 bad	a) looking
2 big-	b) sighted
3 left-	c) fashioned
4 short-	d) tempered
5 good-	e) headed
6 old-	f) handed

2 Then use the words to fill in the gaps in the sentences.

1 My grandmother has to wear glasses because she is so ....

2 I am usually .... but I play the guitar with my right hand.

3 Since my friend came first in the exams, he's got very .... and thinks he's the most intelligent boy in the world.

4 All the girls want to meet my cousin because he's really ....

5 My sister won't wear the clothes she bought last year – she says they're ....

6 When my little sister stays up too late, she gets really ....

4 Lexical cloze

Read the text below and decide which answer A or B best fits each space. There is an example at the beginning (0).

0   A went   B got

MY COUSIN'S WEDDING

When my cousin (0) ...*B*... engaged last year, nobody in our family was surprised. He met his fiancée, Sarah, (1) .... he was on holiday in Greece. They soon (2) .... in love.

They considered getting married straightaway but in the end they decided to be (3) .... and wait for a year. They (4) .... a few rows during that time, but nothing very serious. Then finally, last Saturday, they got married.

We all went to the wedding and, later, to the (5) ...., which was in a big hotel. It was great (6) .... We had a big dinner and then the best man gave a speech and (7) .... lots of jokes. (8) ...., we danced and sang until the early hours of the morning. I'm sure my cousin and his wife will be really happy together.

1	A while		B as	
2	A felt		B fell	
3	A sensitive		B sensible	
4	A had		B made	
5	A reception		B ceremony	
6	A funny		B fun	
7	A did		B made	
8	A Afterwards		B After	

Writing: developing a paragraph ▶ CB pp.29–30

1 Topic sentences

Read the topic sentences in the following composition. Then complete each paragraph by inserting the sentences below in the correct paragraph. You don't need all the sentences.

My Best Friend

My best friend is called Fiona. ....
....

A lot of people think that Fiona is quiet and shy. ....
....

We get on well because we have the same interests and hobbies. ....
....

We're going to go on holiday together next year to Florida. ....
....

I'm really glad I've got a neighbour like Fiona.
....
....

But when you get to know her you realise she's just the opposite.

Fiona's brother is at university and he's studying Tourism.

She's really lively and she's got a great sense of humour.

She's the same age as me and she lives just next door.

She loves Robbie Williams and so do I.

My other best friend is called Sarah and she lives next door.

I'm really keen on swimming and so is she.

We're looking forward to going to Disneyworld and all the places we've read about.

For my last holiday, I went on an adventure holiday in the Alps.

As you can see, I'd really miss her if we ever moved away.

2 Correct a sample answer

A student has written a composition describing her sister, but she has not organised the text into paragraphs.

1 Divide the composition into four paragraphs.
2 Cross out any sentences that do not fit the topic of that paragraph.

When I tell people that there are seven people in my family, they are very surprised because most families in my country are quite small. I love all my family, of course, but Clare, my oldest sister, is really special. Let me tell you why. Clare's very kind and thoughtful, for a start. Last week, for example, I had to stay in bed because I was sick. She spent all her free time with me. She even lent me her mobile phone so I could ring my friends. She's a bit moody sometimes but I don't mind. Another reason I love Clare is because she's great fun. She's always making us laugh with her jokes and with the things she does. Every time she goes out, she brings home a funny story about something she's seen or heard. She is going to be a doctor. To sum up, I'd say that my sister is not just a sister but my best friend too. I'm so lucky to have her. She's the best sister in the world.

▶▶ *writing strategy*

Make sure all the sentences in one paragraph are on the same topic. This will make the text easier for your reader to follow. ◀◀

3 Writing task

Your teacher has asked you to write a composition describing one of your neighbours. Write about 120–180 words.

Remember to:

- brainstorm your ideas. Think of three main areas you want to describe and write headings for each. Then make notes under each heading.

- write a topic sentence at the start of each paragraph. Then develop the paragraph by giving examples and explanations to illustrate your points.

4 Time out

Speaking ▶ CB p.31

Making suggestions

▶▶ *speaking strategy*

When you discuss plans or ideas with a partner, make suggestions and respond to your partner's suggestions. ◀◀

1 It's your best friend David's birthday next week. You and a friend are discussing what to buy him. Put the conversation in the right order.

☐ a) Fine!

☐ b) Good idea! *We could* go tonight.

☐ c) Hi, Ella! I've been looking for you everywhere. It's David's birthday next Saturday! *What can we* get him?

☐ d) No, I don't think that's a good idea. His parents are going to do that.

☐ e) *No, I don't think that's a very good idea.* They're too expensive. *What about* getting him a Björk CD?

☐ f) *No, that's no good,* either. He's got all of her CDs. Anyway, *he's not very keen on* her any more.

☐ g) Hi, John. Yes, I've been thinking what to get David. *What about* a Manchester United shirt? *He's crazy about* football.

☐ h) Oh, isn't he? Well, let me think. I know! *We could* get him something for his computer!

☐ i) Well, in that case, I've got no idea what to get him. Hang on! *What about* asking his brother? Maybe he can help us.

2 Now group the phrases in *italics* under the correct heading. Write them in your notebook.

A Asking for suggestions

B Making suggestions

C Turning down suggestions

D Talking about likes and dislikes

Reading ▶ CB pp.32–33

1 True or false?

Scan the texts on pp.32–33 of your Coursebook and decide if these sentences are true (T) or false (F).

1 Five British kings have lived in The Royal Pavilion. ..*F*...

2 The Royal Pavilion is near the coast. ....

3 If you visit The Royal Pavilion you can see a large collection of wild animals. ....

4 Everyone who visits Longleat gets a free CD. ....

5 The safari park at Longleat is the only one in Britain. ....

6 You can take a boat trip at Longleat. ....

7 At the Museum of London you learn about immigrants who have come to live in the city. ....

8 There are Weekend Workshops in the Museum of London. ....

2 Definitions

Replace the words in *italics* with an appropriate word from the list.

fantasy / fascinating / ingenious / scary / latest / unique

1 The talk that we heard on the secrets of the Universe was *very interesting*. ....

2 Have you seen the *most recent* exhibition in the Science Museum? ....

3 We saw things in the museum that were really *frightening*. ....

4 In the Science Museum we saw many *cleverly designed* 20th century inventions. ....

5 In the studio we saw the *imaginary* world of the future. ....

6 It was great seeing the dinosaur skeleton because it is *the only one of its kind* – there's nothing else like it in the world. ....

3 Prepositions

Fill in the gaps with the correct preposition from the list.

about / outside / in / up / over / of / in / with

1 Visit the Museum of London and find out .... the history of the city.

2 Learn about the city from prehistoric times right .... to the present day.

3 Many people have migrated to London .... the centuries.

4 The museum gives visitors a taste .... life in past centuries.

5 The guide describes some famous murders connected .... the city.

6 Visit the safari park at Longleat and see wild animals .... their natural surroundings.

7 Longleat has the biggest safari park .... Africa.

8 The house is located .... the heart of the countryside.

Grammar ▶ CB p.34, grammar file 9

1 *-ing* or *to*-infinitive?

<u>Underline</u> the correct option in each pair.

1 I can't stand *going / to go* to the dentist's.

2 What did you decide *to buy / buying* your mum for her birthday?

3 We can't afford *to have / having* a holiday this year.

4 My friend suggested *to meet / meeting* outside the cinema.

5 My brother promised *to take / taking* me to the party.

6 Do you miss *to live / living* in the countryside?

7 Our teacher recommended *to buy / buying* a language cassette.

8 My neighbour refused *to turn down / turning down* his radio.

9 I'm thinking of *to take / taking* up a new hobby.

10 My parents expect me *to be / being* home by midnight.

2 Which sentence?

Tick the correct sentence in each pair, a) or b).

1 a) My friend wants that I teach him to swim.
   b) My friend wants me to teach him to swim. ✔

2 a) My coach advised me that I take a break from playing.
   b) My coach advised me to take a break from playing.

3 a) My uncle suggested that I get a computer.
   b) My uncle suggested me to get a computer.

4 a) I expect that our team wins the match.
   b) I expect our team to win the match.

5 a) I hope that you enjoy yourself.
   b) I hope you to enjoy yourself.

6 a) Please remind me to ring Bob when I get home.
   b) Please remind me that I ring Bob when I get home.

3 *-ing* or *to*-infinitive

Fill in the gaps with the correct form of the verb in brackets.

1 I learnt to play the guitar by .... (practise) every day.

2 I'm looking forward to .... (play) volleyball tonight.

3 Would you like .... (go) out with me tomorrow?

4 My friend has asked me .... (spend) the holidays with him.

5 It wasn't worth .... (stay up) to watch the film because I'd seen it before.

6 I've given up .... (try) to ice-skate – I'm hopeless at it!

7 We're hoping .... (visit) Canada next year.

8 It's no use .... (switch) on the computer. It's not working.

9 My friends persuaded me .... (eat) at the burger bar with them.

10 You must remind me .... (feed) the neighbour's dog!

4 **Change of meaning**

**Fill in the gaps with the verb in the *-ing* form
or *to*-infinitive.**

1 *tell*

a) Did you remember .... Mandy that
the party starts at 7 o'clock?

b) I don't remember .... you that you
could use my mobile phone!

2 *meet*

a) I'm never going to forget .... my
favourite singer!

b) I forgot .... my brother at the
station last night. He was furious!

3 *have*

a) I stopped .... music lessons
because they were expensive.

b) We stopped the car .... a short
break.

4 *call*

a) I tried .... you this morning but the
line was busy.

b) If the phone line is busy, I suggest you try
.... again later.

5 *stay*

a) Oh help, is that the time? I didn't mean ....
.... so long – my parents will be furious!

b) I don't want to go to university if it means
.... at home every night!

5 **Extra word**

**One of the following sentences is correct.
Tick it. In each of the other sentences there
is one unnecessary word. Cross it out.**

1 I don't want that my sister to come to the
concert with us.

2 I can't stand to playing kids' games.

3 You would had better wear boots because the
forest is very muddy.

4 I must not forget to buy John a birthday present.

5 My friend suggested me buying the new Celine
Dion CD.

6 My brother keeps in teasing me about my new
girlfriend.

7 I recommend you eating at the new pizza place.

8 My grandparents agreed me to buy a new
computer.

9 My dad's job may involve in working abroad for
a time.

10 I've finished with doing my homework now –
shall we go out?

Vocabulary ▶ CB p.35

1 **-ed / -ing?**

<u>Underline</u> **the correct adjective in each pair.**

1 When I went to the safari park, I was *fascinating / fascinated* by
the giraffes.

2 I've just been to an amusement park and the rides were really
thrilled / thrilling.

3 My friend has an *amazed / amazing* collection of postcards.

4 The guide told us some murder stories and we were really
frightened / frightening!

5 The result of the match was quite *surprised / surprising*.

6 I get so *boring / bored* when I watch football!

7 The audience were *amused / amusing* when the actor sat on his
sword.

8 Losing my wallet was really *annoying / annoyed*!

2 **Verbs + prepositions**

**1 Match a verb from Column A with a preposition from
Column B.**

A	B
1 agree	a) about
2 apologise	b) at
3 prevent	c) for
4 spend	d) from
5 stare	e) of
6 succeed	f) on
7 think	g) with
8 worry	h) in

**2 Fill in the gaps with the correct phrase. Be careful
of tenses!**

1 On this holiday you can just relax – you don't need to
.... anything!

2 How much money did you ....
repairing your computer?

3 I wish that boy wouldn't .... me all the
time. He must think I'm famous or something!

4 My brother thinks football is awful but I don't ....
.... him – I love it.

5 My parents made me .... breaking my
aunt's best vase.

6 They've put a barrier round the lake to .... anyone
.... falling in.

7 What do you .... this year's fashions in
clothes? Do you like them?

8 If I .... passing my exams, my parents
have promised to take me on holiday.

3 Adjectives + prepositions

Underline the correct word in each pair.

1 I'm not very good *in / at* computer games.

2 My brother is mad *about / for* football.

3 Aren't you getting a bit tired *from / of* rollerblading?

4 I'm getting quite interested *on / in* acting and the theatre.

5 When you get bored *at / with* playing that computer game, will you come out with me?

6 Hurry up or we'll be late *at / for* the concert!

7 Why is Harry absent *from / to* school again?

8 Are you afraid *by / of* spiders?

9 Our football coach is expert *on / at* explaining the rules of the game.

10 You mustn't be rude *at / to* the referee or he'll send you off the field!

4 Phrasal verbs with *go*

Fill in the gaps with the correct particle from the list. The definitions are in brackets to help you.

off / back / down with / on / up / in for

1 I like swimming but I never go .... (= *take part in*) competitions.

2 The match went .... (= *continued*) for longer than we expected.

3 My friend can't come on the school trip because she's gone .... (= *caught*) flu.

4 The cost of guitar lessons has gone .... (= *risen*) in price recently.

5 I used to love playing with the computer but I've completely gone .... (= *lost interest in*) it now.

6 If we go .... (= *return*) to the same holiday resort next year, I'm going to try water-skiing.

5 Open cloze

Read the text and think of the word that best fits each space. Use only one word in each space. There is an example at the beginning (0).

SCUBA DIVING

My friend is really mad **(0)** ....*about*.... scuba diving. He spends all his money **(1)** .... equipment and lessons. His parents don't really approve **(2)** .... his hobby. They worry **(3)** .... him and his school work. They would prefer him **(4)** .... spend more time studying. But Ben doesn't pay much attention to what they say. He says he'll think **(5)** .... his exams next year, but not now. He's interested **(6)** .... joining one of the big clubs but he needs to be really expert **(7)** .... scuba diving before he can do that. He's very determined so I expect he'll go **(8)** .... practising until he's a champion.

Writing: grammatical links ► CB pp.37–38

Grammatical reference links

Remember that we can use reference words like *it, here, this, that* and *them* to link ideas together.

1 *I live in Madrid. **It's** the capital of Spain.*

2 *My town's famous. Many people come **here**.*

3 *The market is in Bread Street. **This** is in the old quarter of the city.*

4 *The city centre is very busy on Saturday. **That** means parking is difficult.*

5 *The art gallery has paintings by Van Gogh. Lots of tourists come to see **them**.*

---

1 Reference links

Fill in the gaps with one suitable word (e.g. *this, that, them, here*, etc.).

1 My town's quite famous so lots of tourists come ...*here*....... in summer. We're always glad to see .... They make .... town more lively. Also, when they spend .... money in .... town, it helps local businesses.

2 There is a big fish market every Friday. .... market sells every kind of fish you can imagine.

3 Winter is great here because .... is the skiing season and lots of people come .... to take part.

4 There is an ancient wall round the town. You can walk right round .... if you want. .... was probably built about 900 years ago.

5 Every year, in February, ... is a festival in the town. .... celebrates the coming of spring. All the inhabitants take part in .... festival.

2 Correct a sample answer

A teacher asked her class to write a composition describing their home town. Read the sample composition that one student wrote. Unfortunately, she did not use many reference words. Write the composition out again in your notebook, putting in reference words where necessary.

My Home Town

The town I live in is great because the town is only 6 kilometres from the coast. I was born in the town so I know the town and its inhabitants very well. Let me describe the town.

Visitors to my town are usually amazed at how old the buildings are. If you look closely, you will see that the buildings date back to Medieval times. Everywhere, there are narrow little streets. In summer, the streets are full of tourists but at other times of the year the streets are very quiet.

My town is very colourful too. There are markets on most days. The markets are always very busy and are popular with the tourists who come to buy from the markets. There is a bull-fighting ring in the centre of the town. The bull-fighting ring isn't used for bull fights any more but a lot of concerts and festivals take place in the centre of town every year.

Last but not least, I must mention the activities you can do here. The activities are famous all over the country. You can do all sorts of beach sports but there are lots of theatres, parks, cinemas and discos, too.

To sum up, my town is a fantastic place to be. I feel really lucky to live in my town and I never want to leave.

3 Writing task

Your teacher has asked you to write a composition about a place of interest which you have visited with your parents. Write about 120–180 words.

Remember to:

- use reference words in appropriate places to avoid unnecessary repetition.
- use linking expressions like *First of all, ...,* and *Last but not least, ...* to link points or whole paragraphs to each other.
- check your grammar and spelling when you have finished.

Progress check 1

Grammar

1 Present tenses

Fill in the gaps with the correct form of the verb in brackets.

1 I .... (think) of going to the USA next year.
2 .... (you/know) who this book .... (belong) to?
3 Look! Those men .... (make) a film.
4 Where .... (you/plan) to spend your next holiday?
5 You .... (look) scared. What's the matter?
6 I'm sorry but I .... (not/understand) what you .... (mean).
7 I .... (see) Paul every day but I still .... (not/know) where he .... (live).
8 Martha can't come to the phone because she .... (have) a bath.

2 Frequency adverbs

Put the words into the correct order to make questions and sentences. Write them in your notebook.

1 always before do evening go homework I in my out the I
2 a disco during go never the to We week
3 a help housework I Mum once or the twice week with
4 usually brother come dinner doesn't for home My
5 Do early get on Saturdays up usually you?
6 again and cinema friends go I and My now the to
7 don't go often on shopping Sundays We
8 time to from go grandparents I my stay time to with

3 Present perfect or past simple?

Underline the correct option in each pair.

1 The plane *has landed/landed* at 6 o'clock.
2 Sorry I'm late. *Have you been waiting/Have you waited* long?
3 My Dad *bought/has bought* me a video camera for my last birthday but I *didn't learn/haven't learnt* how to use it yet.
4 I *tried/have tried* a lot of sports but I *never went/I've never been* sailing before.
5 My friend *has bought/has been buying* two tickets for the football match.
6 *I've been learning/I've learnt* how to play the guitar but I'm not very good yet.
7 I bought Jim a Britney Spears album but he *has already got/he's already been getting* it.
8 I'm afraid I *never heard/have never heard* of Florence Nightingale. Who was she?

4 *for, since, ago* or *in*?

Fill in the gaps with the correct time expression.

1 We've been in class .... an hour.
2 The train left five minutes ....
3 It's a week .... I saw him.
4 How long .... did it happen?
5 The film starts .... two minutes.
6 I've lived here .... I was born.
7 We've been waiting .... ages.

5 Past tenses

Use the prompts to write a story.

1 Angela / jump / out / bed / and / look / out of the window.
....

2 The sun / shine / and last night's storm / disappear.
....

3 She / get dressed / quickly / and / run / downstairs.
....

4 The suitcases, which she / pack / the night before, were by the front door.
....

5 She / still eat / breakfast / when the doorbell / ring.
....

6 A group of her friends / stand / on the doorstep.
....

7 'Hurry up, Angela,' they / call. 'We don't want to miss the plane.'
....

8 She / take / a deep breath. She / look forward to / this day / for months. Now it / finally / arrive.
....

6 -ing form or infinitive?

Four sentences are correct. Tick them. <u>Underline</u> the mistakes in the other sentences and correct them.

1 Do you like watching sport on TV? ....

2 I must stop to bite my nails. ....

3 I'd love to meet Steven Spielberg. ....

4 I'm looking forward to hear from you. ....

5 It's no use to phone – Tom is out all day. ....

6 I don't want to miss my plane. ....

7 Sue keeps to lose things. ....

8 It's not worth to get a taxi. I live right next to the station.
....

9 You must remind me to book tickets for the concert.
....

10 I can't stand to travel by coach. ....

Vocabulary

7 Verbs + prepositions + -ing

Use a preposition from Box A and a verb from Box B to fill in the gaps, making any changes necessary. You will need to use some prepositions more than once.

A	about	at	for	from	in	of	with

B	buy	look	after	fall	lose	pass	practise	win
	reach	see	work					

1 I'm thinking .... a new motorbike.

2 Her parents tried to stop her .... her boyfriend.

3 My dad's fed up .... in an office.

4 The teacher praised me .... my exams.

5 The explorers succeeded .... the South Pole.

6 I love playing the cello and I never get bored ....

7 A true sportsperson is good .... as well as winning.

8 I want to be a nurse and specialise .... sick children.

9 I'm very proud .... a gold medal for swimming.

10 My sister won't go horse-riding because she's afraid .... off her horse!

8 Choosing the right word

<u>Underline</u> the correct word in each pair.

1 Don't forget *for / about* the party!

2 Let's *take / do* a break.

3 I've *done / made* a lot of new friends.

4 We're all going to take *place / part* in the concert.

5 My brother's got a really interesting *job / work*.

6 When are you going *in / on* holiday?

7 The price of each ticket has increased from $5 *at / to* $6.

8 I'm tired *as / so* I think I'll go to bed.

9 We often *do / go* jogging on Saturday mornings.

10 I'm glad my team *won / beat* the match.

9 Word formation

1 Follow the instructions below. Write the words in your notebook.

1 Make adjectives from these verbs:
a) *think* b) *differ* c) *cheer* d) *attract* e) *surprise*

2 Make adjectives from these nouns:
a) *boredom* b) *fascination* c) *intelligence*
d) *interest* e) *surprise*

2 Use the word in CAPITALS at the end of each sentence to form an adjective that fits in the gap.

1 I thought the film was really .... EXCITE

2 Dave always looks happy and .... CHEER

3 Sonya is the most .... girl in the class. INTELLIGENCE

4 I never get .... with watching football. BORE

5 My sister's hobbies are quite .... from mine. DIFFER

6 Astronomy is a really .... subject. INTEREST

7 My girlfriend is very .... ATTRACT

8 I was .... by the ending of the film. SURPRISE

5 Ambitions

Speaking ▶ CB p.41

1 Jobs

Fill in the gaps with a correct verb from the list.

carries / designs / tests / bakes / performs / repairs / prosecutes or defends / serves

1 A lawyer .... people in court.

2 A plumber .... toilets and water pipes.

3 A surgeon .... operations in hospital.

4 A flight attendant .... drinks and food on a plane.

5 A porter .... suitcases and bags.

6 An optician .... people's sight.

7 An architect .... new buildings and bridges.

8 A baker .... bread and cakes.

2 Describing personal qualities

Make adjectives from the nouns in CAPITALS to fit the gaps in the sentences.

1 Medicine is a demanding career so you need to be extremely ......*dedicated*........ to succeed. DEDICATION

2 My sister is really .... and wants to run her own company one day. AMBITION

3 To get to the top in business, you have to be very .... COMPETITION

4 I'm lazy – I'm just not .... enough to be a professional sportsperson. ENERGY

5 If you are .... and like writing plays and fiction, you may like to consider a career as a screenwriter. IMAGINATION

6 You need a .... mind if you want a career in law. LOGIC

7 You need to be quite .... if you want to teach small children. PRACTICALITY

8 You need to be patient and .... if you want a career in nursing. CARE

3 Comparing photos

Look at the photos. Underline the correct option in each pair.

(1) *In / On* the first picture, I (2) *can / could* see a scientist. She (3) *wears / is wearing* special glasses and gloves and she (4) *holds / is holding* a little bottle of something – maybe it's a dangerous liquid. (5) *In / On* the second picture (6) *it / there* is a rock singer. I think she's on stage or maybe in a TV studio (7) *because / so* there are bright lights behind her (8) *and / also* she (9) *wears / is wearing* a microphone.

I (10) *think / mean* a singer's job is more interesting. A singer (11) *travels / is travelling* round the world and (12) *meets / is meeting* all sorts of interesting people. The life of a rock star is very glamorous and if you're lucky you can earn a lot of money.

A scientist usually has to work in a laboratory (13) *as / so* she is not so free. I mean, a scientist discovers useful things but the job is harder. She has to work in the same place with the same people every day. I don't mean it's not an important job – it may be more important than the singer. But for me, I would rather be a singer. There are more advantages, (14) *in / from* my opinion.

Reading ▶ CB pp.42–43

1 Unfamiliar words

Complete the sentences with words from the list.

coincidence / convinced / waste / prediction / compatible / obsessed / stubborn / vague

1 I don't believe in horoscopes – I think they're a .... of time.

2 It's difficult to persuade a .... person to change his/her mind about something.

3 When people have a good relationship because they share the same interests, we say they are ....

4 People who are .... with an idea never think of anything else.

5 My plans are very .... – I wish they were more definite.

6 By ...., our next-door neighbours have booked the same holiday as us!

7 The fortune teller made a .... but it never came true.

8 Alicia is .... that her horoscope is right but I'm not so sure.

2 Prepositions

Underline the correct word in each pair.

1 Do you believe *on / in* fate?

2 Are you interested *in / on* knowing what your stars say?

3 Some people say astrology is a science but I don't agree *to / with* them.

4 I'm going to keep *in / on* reading my horoscope – but just for fun!

5 Some people believe anything and astrologers take advantage *in / of* that.

6 Who was that man you were talking *at / to*?

3 Words that go together

Fill in the gaps with the correct form of a verb from the list.

come / date / do / keep / make / avoid

1 When was the last time you had to .... a *big decision*?

2 My dreams would .... *true* if I could meet Robbie Williams!

3 Do you ever use the Internet to .... *research* for school projects?

4 My horoscope helps me to .... *unpleasant events*.

5 My brother has started to .... *a girl* he met on holiday and he says he's in love!

6 If you want to remember things, it's a good idea to .... *a diary*.

Grammar ▶ CB p.44, grammar file 8

1 *will* or present continuous?

Underline the correct option in each pair.

1 **A:** What would you like to eat?
   B: *I'm having / I'll have* a burger and chips, please.

2 **A:** Is your brother still going out with that girl?
   B: Yes, haven't you heard? They *will get / are getting* married next year!

3 **A:** Let's go to the cinema!
   B: Sorry, *I'll meet / I'm meeting* my boyfriend tonight.

4 **A:** I can't lift this suitcase.
   B: Wait! *I'll do / I'm doing* it for you.

5 **A:** It's decided! *We're having / We'll have* a party next week.
   B: Great news! *I'm bringing / I'll bring* my CDs!

2 will/shall or going to?

Fill in the gaps with the correct form of the verb in brackets.

A: Hello, Jane. I hear you're going on holiday!

B: Yes, I'm off to Russia! I (1) .... (spend) two weeks there! I (2) .... (stay) with some friends of my parents.

A: You lucky thing!

B: I know. What about you?

A: Well, I'm not sure but I think I (3) .... (probably/get) a holiday job. I (4) .... (study) medicine next year, you know, so I need to save some money first.

B: What sort of job would you like?

A: I don't know. Maybe I (5) .... (work) on a farm.

B: I don't think they pay very well!

A: No, I (6) .... (probably/not/ earn) very much. But I don't know what else I can do.

B: Why not look in the local newspaper? I'm going to the shops now. (7) .... I .... (buy) you one?

A: Yes, please. That's a great idea!

3 Which future?

Tick the correct sentence in each pair.

1 a) I'm going to the doctor's tomorrow. I've got an appointment.
   b) I'll go to the doctor's tomorrow. I've got an appointment.

2 a) Is that the phone? I'll answer it!
   b) Is that the phone? I'm going to answer it!

3 a) Look at the clouds! It will rain.
   b) Look at the clouds! It's going to rain.

4 a) I promise I'll be careful.
   b) I promise I'm going to be careful.

5 a) I can't meet you tonight. I'll wash my hair.
   b) I can't meet you tonight. I'm washing my hair.

6 a) My friend's coming to my house tonight. We arranged it yesterday.
   b) My friend will come to my house tonight. We arranged it yesterday.

4 Find the mistake

There is a tense mistake in each of these sentences. <u>Underline</u> it and write the sentences correctly in your notebook. Sometimes more than one answer is possible.

1 Remember to phone me as soon as you'll arrive.

2 I'm not sure what to do this weekend. Perhaps I'm staying at home.

3 I've arranged to meet Paul tonight. We'll go to the cinema.

4 That bag looks heavy. Am I helping you?

5 Do you want a cold drink? I'm getting you one from the fridge.

6 Will you do anything special tonight? If not, why not come out with me?

7 When I'll get home, I think I'll spend some time on the computer.

8 I promise I'm paying you back the money you lent me.

9 It's very cold! It's snowing later, I'm sure.

10 It's Mum's birthday next month. She's being 45!

5 Transformations

Complete the second sentence so that it has a similar meaning to the first sentence, using the word given. Do not change the word given. Use between two and five words.

1 We've arranged a meeting for tomorrow.
   going
   We .... a meeting tomorrow.

2 What time is the plane scheduled to take off?
   does
   What time .... off?

3 It's late so would you like a lift in my car?
   I
   It's late so .... a lift in my car?

4 I have a dentist's appointment at 2 p.m. today.
   to
   I .... the dentist's at 2 p.m. today.

5 The film is about to begin.
   in
   The film .... a few minutes.

6 My sister intends to study archaeology at university.
   to
   My sister .... archaeology at university.

Vocabulary ▶ CB p.45

1 Choosing the right word

Complete the sentences below with the correct word. Use each word once only.

> sheet   form

1 I need another .... of writing paper.
2 You need to fill in an application .... for the job.

> win   earn

3 Lawyers .... large salaries.
4 I hope I .... the lottery.

> experience   experiment

5 We did an interesting .... in our Chemistry lesson.
6 At our school, 16-year-olds do four weeks' work ....

> resignation   retirement

7 My grandfather is a pensioner and is really enjoying his ....
8 Paul handed in his .... because he was bored with his job.

2 Prepositions

Fill in the gaps with the correct preposition from the list.

on / as / at / for / with / at / on / for / on

1 I'm going to share a flat .... my cousin while I'm .... university.
2 My dad starts work .... a new engineering project next week.
3 He works very hard – it's 10 p.m. and he's still .... work!
4 Mum's away .... business this weekend, so I can do what I like!
5 The airline has invited my sister to go .... an interview.
6 My last teacher worked .... a football referee in his holidays.
7 Do you want to work for a big company or would you rather work .... yourself?
8 I'd rather go .... holiday than get a summer job!

3 Which part of speech?

Look at each of the words in bold and decide if it is a noun (n.) or an adjective (adj.).

1 You're **unlikely** to get a job as an air steward if you don't speak English. *adj.*
2 Astrologers charge a lot of money for their **predictions**. ....
3 My sister is extremely **disorganised** so she wouldn't make a good lawyer. ....
4 The boy I met at my interview was rather **unfriendly**. ....
5 In an **emergency**, I can phone my father at work. ....
6 My brother is too **disobedient** to be a soldier. ....
7 When I need **advice**, I talk to my friends. ....

4 Opposites

Make each of the adjectives below negative, then put it in the correct column.

hope / important / organised / legal / use / legible / mature / obedient / probable / reliable

im-	il-	un-
1	3	5 ....
2	4	6 ....
dis-	**-less**	
7	9 *hopeless*	
8	10	

5 Word formation

1 Read the text below. Then decide whether you need a positive or negative adjective. The words in *italics* should help you decide.

0 It is *illegal* to drive a car *without* a driving licence. LEGALISE
1 The mother *punished* her child for being .... OBEDIENCE
2 My watch is old *but* it's still very .... RELY
3 If you want *to work as a stuntman* you must be completely .... FEAR
4 Flight attendants need to be .... because they *work irregular hours*. FLEXIBILITY
5 People who say they don't believe in astrology *but* insist on reading their horoscopes are being .... LOGIC
6 The applicant *didn't* have the necessary qualifications so he was .... for the job. FITNESS
7 Chris will be a fine actor in a few years *but* he's still a bit .... at the moment. MATURITY

2 Now fill in the missing words. Use the word in CAPITALS at the end of each sentence to form a word that fits in the gap. There is an example at the beginning (0).

Writing: formal letter ▶ CB pp.47–48

1 Formal or informal?

▶▶ *writing strategy*

Before you start to write a letter, always check who is going to read it and decide whether your language should be formal or informal. Do **not** write a mixture of formal and informal language.

◀◀

Tick the formal items in this list.

1 Write soon,
2 I would be available to start the job as soon as I am needed.
3 I'm looking forward to hearing from you.
4 I'd be OK at this job because …
5 I want more details about your job ad.
6 I get on great with people.
7 Believe me, I'd make a fabulous guide.
8 I'm writing about the advertisement you put in yesterday's newspaper.
9 I can start anytime – no problem.
10 I feel I would be suitable for this job because …
11 Yours,
12 Yours sincerely,
13 I would have no difficulty dealing with groups of young people.
14 I've got a good deal of experience in this area.

2 Correct a sample answer

Read the task on p.48 of your Coursebook and look at this sample answer. Unfortunately, some of the words and phrases the student has used are too informal. The teacher has underlined them. Write the letter out in your notebook, replacing the informal words and phrases with more formal ones.

3 Writing task

You have seen the following advertisement in your local paper.

Students!

Are you looking for a holiday job?
Are you energetic, patient, and good with children?
Can you speak English?

•

We need young people to help run our children's summer camps. Many of the children (aged 8 – 12) come from overseas.
Apply in writing to the address below, telling us about yourself and why you think you would be suitable for this job. Please let us know when you are available.

Mrs P Smith, Sunshine Holidays, PO Box 2950

Write a letter of application in 120–180 words.

Remember to:

- set your letter out correctly.
- use formal language.
- edit your letter carefully.

Dear Sir,

I've just seen your <u>ad.</u> in the paper and I want to be a tour guide.

I am 16 years old and I'm a student. I go to Clarksville High School in the centre of the city. I've been going there for six years and I'm hoping to go to university in two years' time, to study law. I'm <u>crazy about</u> sport and I belong to <u>millions of</u> clubs. My favourite hobby is swimming. I get on <u>great</u> with people of my age and I've got lots of friends. I speak very good English.

I think I'd make a good tour guide because I know this area <u>like the back of my hand.</u> I've lived in this city all my life and I know quite a lot about the history. I'd really enjoy showing other young people around all the famous places. I'm good at dealing with problems and emergencies and I bet this would be useful too.

The school year finishes in June so I could start work then.

<u>Do write soon,</u>

<u>Best wishes,</u>

Patrick

Speaking ▶ CB p.49

Describing and speculating

▶▶ *speaking strategy*

When you are describing a photo, remember to use the *present continuous tense* to describe people's actions.

◀◀

Look at the pictures and read the descriptions. Some sentences have factual mistakes in them. <u>Underline</u> them and write the sentences out correctly in your notebook.

A

Picture A

The people in the first picture are having a good day out. They look much happier than the people in the second picture. In the foreground, I can see a man and two young people. They're riding on a sort of train and they're getting very wet. The woman looks a bit scared. The boy sitting in front of the woman is wearing a helmet. There's a man standing nearby and he's holding some sandwiches. Maybe he's the boy's father. There's a woman standing behind him. She looks like their grandmother. In the background, there are lots of people lying on the grass. They're having picnics and enjoying themselves.

B

Picture B

The people in the second picture are probably feeling annoyed. The woman is sitting at the check-in desk. I can see from her face that she's angry. The man next to her might be her husband. He's sitting on a seat. He looks amused. There's a little boy sitting on the floor playing a banjo. He's dressed in a suit. There are two girls watching him. They look bored. In the background, there are lots more passengers. They look extremely excited.

Reading ▶ CB pp.50–51

1 Body language

Match each of the phrases to a picture.

1 He's nodding. ....
2 He's shrugging. ....
3 He's rubbing his ear. ....
4 He's folding his arms across his chest. ....
5 He's leaning forward. ....
6 He's tilting his head on one side. ....
7 He's putting his hand over his mouth. ....
8 He's winking. ....
9 He's shaking his fist. ....
10 He's crossing his legs. ....

2 Choosing the right word

<u>Underline</u> the correct word in each pair.

1 People *lift / raise* their eyebrows when they are surprised.
2 Fred *nodded / shook* his head in agreement.
3 The boy didn't know the answer so he just *shrugged / hugged*.
4 The teacher *frowned / grinned* in annoyance.
5 If you *lean / fold* your arms across your chest, people will think you're being stubborn.
6 Louise felt ashamed of what she had done and *hung / dropped* her head.

Grammar ▶ CB p.52, grammar file 11

1 Zero / first conditional

Fill in the gaps with the correct form of the verb in brackets.

1 I .... (always / blush) if I .... (get) embarrassed.
2 If Lucy .... (ring), ... (tell) her I'll be back soon.
3 If I .... (see) John tonight, I .... (tell) him the news.
4 I .... (not / be able to) buy a mobile phone unless Dad .... (give) me the money.
5 .... (shake) your head if you .... (not / agree) with what I'm saying.
6 Unless you .... (talk) about your problems, nobody .... (be able to) help you.
7 If you .... (send) Tom an e-mail, he .... (be) really pleased.
8 We .... (have) a barbecue in the garden tonight unless it .... (rain).

2 Sentence completion

Tick the correct option, a) or b).

1 I'd buy a motorbike …
   a) if I would have enough money.
   b) if I had enough money. ✔
2 I wouldn't blush …
   a) if people don't tease me.
   b) if people didn't tease me.
3 My hands shake …
   a) if I were nervous.
   b) if I am nervous.
4 If I had a mobile phone, …
   a) I will phone you.
   b) I would phone you.

5 Make sure you lock the door …
  a) if you go out.
  b) if you will go out.

6 Unless you tell your parents where you're going, …
  a) they'll be worried.
  b) they won't be worried.

3 Which conditional?

Match the sentence halves to make logical sentences.

A	B
1 I'll win a lot of money	a) I'd be delighted.
2 I would tell the truth	b) if I spoke more languages.
3 If you disagree with me,	c) if my friends forgot my birthday.
4 Don't go on the Internet so often	d) if you want to save money.
5 You will be punished	e) if I were you.
6 I could get a job abroad	f) please tell me.
7 If my parents bought me a Gameboy,	g) unless you apologise.
8 I'd be furious	h) if I come first in the competition.

4 Open cloze

Read the text and think of the word that best fits each space. Use only one word in each space. There is an example at the beginning (0).

DESERT ISLAND

Imagine you had **(0)** ..*to*... spend six months alone on a small island. Which luxury object would you take with **(1)** ....? Would you take a bicycle, for example, or maybe **(2)** .... mobile phone? Personally, I would take a computer. Computers are practical **(3)** .... educational. They're good fun, too! If I **(4)** .... a computer on my island, I could **(5)** .... games, and send e-mails to all **(6)** .... friends. If I **(7)** .... lonely, I could join a chat room and talk to people with similar interests. And **(8)** .... life on my island got too depressing, I could surf the Internet and find ideas on how to escape.

Vocabulary ▶ CB p.53

1 Adverbs

Make adverbs from the adjectives at the end of the sentences to fill in the gaps.

1 John Lennon's death was .... sad. TERRIBLE

2 Ian Fleming's hero, James Bond, liked driving .... FAST

3 Mother Teresa was an .... saintly woman. EXTREME

4 My cousin knows Tom Cruise quite ....! GOOD

5 The President spoke .... to the photographers who were annoying him. ANGRY

6 I'm .... sorry but I've lost the *Famous People* book you lent me. AWFUL

2 Adjective or adverb?

Fill in the gaps with the correct adverb.

1 **hard / hardly**
  a) Speak up! I can .... hear you!
  b) I worked really .... last term.

2 **quick / quickly**
  a) If you're going to the shops, please be ....!
  b) My father drives very ....

3 **awful / awfully**
  a) The exam was .... difficult.
  b) My hair feels .... – I must wash it!

4 **real / really**
  a) If that coat is made of .... fur, I don't want it.
  b) I'm .... sorry for what happened.

5 **happy / happily**
  a) The prince and princess lived .... ever after.
  b) I'm so .... to meet you!

6 **late / lately**
  a) The bus is .... again!
  b) Barcelona have been playing really well ....

3 Modifying adjectives

Fill in the gaps with *extremely* or *absolutely*.

1 The news was .... fantastic.

2 Computer genius Bill Gates is .... rich.

3 The weather was .... awful.

4 I was .... worried about what happened.

5 The book was .... interesting.

6 We had an .... fabulous holiday.

7 The bride was clearly .... happy.

8 The horror film was .... terrifying.

4 Word formation

1 Complete the tables.

Verb	Adjective	Noun
1 *amaze*	2 *amazing*	amazement
enjoy	3	4
annoy	5	6
7	acceptable	8
astonish	9	10

Adjective	Adverb	Noun
11	12	fluency
patient	13	14
envious	15	16
17	18	care
happy	19	20
confident	21	22
23	politely	24

2 Read the sentences and underline which type of word is missing from the options given in brackets. Then use the words given in CAPITALS below to form a word that fits each gap.

1 Actor Antonio Banderas can speak English ....
(noun / adverb)

2 Paul's mistake caused him a lot of ....
(adjective / noun)

3 George W. Bush greeted the ambassador with great
.... (noun / adverb)

4 People stared at Michael Jackson in ....
(adjective / noun)

5 Spanish people speak extremely ....
(adjective / adverb)

6 The tourist sighed with .... because nobody
would help him. (adverb / noun)

7 The tourist guide didn't sound very ....
(adjective / adverb)

8 Mobile phones are .... useful. (noun / adverb)

1	FLUENT	5	QUICK
2	EMBARRASS	6	ANNOY
3	POLITE	7	CONFIDENCE
4	AMAZE	8	EXTREME

5 Lexical cloze

! tip

Read the whole text first. Then it will be easier to fill in the gaps correctly.

Read the text below and decide which answer A, B or C best fits each space. There is an example at the beginning (0).

0   **A** arrive   **B** arrival   **C** arriving

GOOD MANNERS ON THE NET

Since the **(0)** ..*B*... of the Internet, written English has become the world's **(1)** .... modern form of communication. But the English used in e-mail and text messages is often **(2)** .... different from normal written English. E-mailers often use abbreviations, such as AFAIC (as far as I'm concerned) and YYSSW (yeah, yeah, sure, sure, whatever).

And the Net has its own symbols that express feeling. If you want to say 'I feel **(3)** .... ', you can just use this symbol, ☺. This is OK between friends, but if you are writing **(4)** ...., you need to use a **(5)** .... casual style. Never write messages in capital letters, for example. It's the Internet equivalent of shouting.

Always think **(6)** .... before you send your message. If you don't use the **(7)** .... forms, the person who receives your message may end up feeling **(8)** .... angry.

1	**A** most	**B** best		**C** more
2	**A** absolutely	**B** very		**C** hardly
3	**A** happy	**B** happily		**C** happiness
4	**A** formal	**B** formality		**C** formally
5	**A** less	**B** little		**C** such
6	**A** careful	**B** carelessly		**C** carefully
7	**A** rightly	**B** correctly		**C** correct
8	**A** absolutely	**B** utterly		**C** extremely

Writing: informal transactional letter

▶ CB pp.55–56

1 Giving advice

Put the words and phrases below into the correct column.

> **! tip**
>
> In transactional letters, you may have to give your opinion or advise someone what to do. Make sure you know the correct phrases to use.

however, …	As I see it, …
in my opinion	you should …
but …	On the other hand
you ought to …	It seems to me that …
nevertheless, …	If I were you, I would …

Advice	Contrast	Opinion
1	1	1 ....
2	2	2 ....
3	3	3 ....
	4	

2 Correct a sample answer

Read the writing task on p.56 of your Coursebook and look at this sample letter. Unfortunately, the student has made a number of mistakes, which the teacher has <u>underlined</u>. Write the letter correctly in your notebook.

WW	<u>Hi</u> Carla!
G/T	It was great to hear that <u>you come</u> to England this summer. You asked what I thought about the courses, so here's my advice.
G	The adventure course <u>sound</u> fantastic. You can do lots of
SP/WW	exciting <u>activity</u> there. Staying at a youth centre might be <u>funny</u>,
∧	too. I think you'd have ∧ great time.
WW/WW	On the other <u>way</u>, painting <u>it's</u> your favourite hobby. I think
GT/GT	you'd enjoy <u>to learn</u> about famous painters and <u>to see</u> their work. Staying in a London hotel would be a big adventure, too. You can go and visit all the famous buildings and enjoy the nightlife.
SP/WW	The <u>choise</u> is really difficult! However, I think you <u>must</u> go on the Art course. You can do activities anywhere but the Art course is special, I think.
	Let me know what you decide!
WW	<u>Yours sincerely.</u>
	Angus

3 Writing task

Your friend Peter has won a writing competition. For his prize, he has to choose between two places. He has written to ask your advice. Read his letter and the descriptions he has sent with them. Then write your reply, giving your advice. Write about 120–180 words.

> I'm sending you a description of the two places. I can go to either of them for 10 days. Travel and accommodation is free. Which do you think I should take? Should I go to the USA or. London?

> **AMERICAN DREAM**
> You will have a great time here in Camp Florida, USA. You will sleep in a tent under the stars. You can swim, surf, go climbing – and much, much more. Includes a trip to Disneyland.

> **THE LONDON EXPERIENCE**
> Stay in a luxury hotel in this exciting capital city. Visit all the famous sights, art galleries and museums. Shop in London's top stores. Visit famous nightspots, including London's top musicals and rock shows.

Remember to:

- make a plan before you start.
- make sure you answer the question in full.
- use the language of advice.
- state your opinion and the reasons for it clearly.

Correction code		
G	=	grammar
SP	=	spelling
P	=	punctuation
WW	=	wrong word
T	=	wrong tense
∧	=	word missing

7 Your health

Speaking ▶ CB p.57

1 Find the mistake

Two students are planning a barbecue. There are mistakes in five of the questions. <u>Underline</u> them and write the questions correctly in your notebook.

A: When do you think should we have the barbecue?

B: Well, we could have it next Saturday. The school holidays begin then.

A: Good idea! Now, we have to think about food. What kind of things we should cook?

B: We could have burgers and sausages.

A: But what's about the vegetarians?

A: Oh yes, I forgot. Don't you think should we do fish instead of sausages?

B: Good idea. Now, what we shall have for dessert?

A: Maybe we could have some kind of gateau?

B: Yes, that sounds great. We've decided then. We'll have burgers and fish, and gateau for dessert, right?

A: Fine. I agree.

2 Words for quantity

1 Match the quantity words in Column A with the food items in Column B. Use each word once only.

A	B
1 a can	a) pasta, chips
2 a carton	b) bread
3 a jar	c) toast, cake
4 a loaf	d) jam
5 a piece / slice	e) milk
6 a portion	f) Coke

2 Fill in the gaps with an appropriate word. You sometimes need to make the word plural.

1 Would you like another .... of cake?

2 I can't open this .... of strawberry jam.

3 Can you go to the shop and buy me three .... of Coke, please?

4 I got a fresh .... of bread from the baker's.

5 In the supermarket, they sell milk in ...., not glass bottles.

6 Put a burger and a small .... of chips on each plate, please.

Reading ▶ CB pp.58–59

1 Text summary

The following paragraph summarises the text on p.58 of your Coursebook. Fill in the gaps with words from the list.

brain / energy / chew / give up / hungry / junk / protein / variety

Eating (1) .... food is not a good idea because it is not healthy. It is better for you to eat a wide (2) .... of food, such as salad, vegetables or cheese. Eat slowly and (3) .... your food properly, otherwise your (4) .... won't register that you've eaten and you'll still feel (5) .... Sugary foods are bad for you so you should (6) .... sweets, biscuits and cake. Foods like chicken and fish contain (7) .... and are much more nutritious. They provide you with the (8) .... to exercise better.

2 Linking words

Complete the sentences below with the correct word. Use each word once only.

so	because	as

1 You should eat protein rich foods .... they're nutritious.

2 You need to eat slowly, ... make time to sit down and eat at the table.

3 You should eat fish and chicken rather than junk food .... it's much healthier.

although	but	however

4 Sugary snacks are tempting .... they're bad for your mind and your body.

5 Sweets and cake give you energy. ...., the energy is short-lived.

6 .... fast food is convenient, it's not good for your health.

3 Choosing the right word

Underline the correct word in each pair.

1 Our mouths are very *sensible/sensitive* to the taste of food.

2 The meal we had last night was very *satisfied/satisfying*.

3 I've been away from home for six weeks and I *lose/miss* my mother's cooking!

4 I started a diet a few days ago but it didn't *last/keep* long!

5 Would you like a *piece/portion* of cake?

6 If you want to eat out, I *recommend/advise* the Chinese restaurant – it is excellent!

4 Words that go together

Fill in the gaps with a verb from the list.

feel / have / make / pay / resist / take

1 If you .... *exercise*, you won't get fat.

2 Let's .... *dinner* in front of the TV tonight!

3 I shouldn't have eaten so much cake but I just couldn't .... the *temptation*.

4 If you want to get fit, you must .... *attention* to your diet.

5 I've eaten too much and now I .... really *sleepy*.

6 Even busy athletes have to .... *time* in their schedule to eat properly!

Grammar ▶ CB p.60, grammar file 20

1 Relative pronouns

Complete the second sentence in each pair with a relative clause, using a word from the list.

who / whose / which / where

1 I walked home with a boy. His parents own a Chinese restaurant.
  I walked home with the boy ....
  ....

2 That's the pizza place. It sells the best food in town.
  That's the pizza place ....
  ....

3 That's the coffee bar. I usually meet my friends there.
  That's the coffee bar ....
  ....

4 I saw a programme about the men. They opened Planet Hollywood.
  I saw a programme about the men ....
  ....

2 Find the mistake

There is a mistake in each of these sentences. Underline it and write the sentences correctly in your notebook.

1 I love the pizzas <u>what</u> my mother makes.
  I love the pizzas (that/which) my mother makes.

2 The magazine who I bought has some good recipes in it.

3 The man I spoke to him was a chef.

4 That's the restaurant that it has a really big garden at the back.

5 That's the boy who's mother was on TV last night.

6 Can you describe the place where you ate there last night?

7 The waiter who served us he wasn't very polite.

8 My parents took all my friends out for a meal, it was really nice of them.

3 Prepositions

Fill in the gaps with an appropriate preposition.

1 The pizza place (which) my friend took me .... was very good.

2 The chair (that) I was sitting .... was really uncomfortable!

3 The hotel (which) we stayed .... was fantastic.

4 The music (that) we listened .... was heavy metal.

5 The paintings (that) we looked .... were great.

6 Members of the club (which) I belong .... are organising a summer party.

7 The boy (that) I spoke .... invited me to a barbecue.

8 I found the wallet (that) I was looking .... under the table!

Relative pronouns

Remember that we can omit relative pronouns when they are the object of the sentence. Where appropriate, put dependent prepositions at the end of the relative clause:

The man was the chef. I spoke to him.

*The man (**who**) I spoke to was the chef.*

---

4 Non-defining relative clauses

Complete the following sentences with a relative pronoun using the information in the box below.

THE HISTORY OF MCDONALD'S

1 In 1954 Ray Kroc, ...*who was an American salesman*........, had an idea that would make him very rich.

2 He invested his cash, ... in a contract to sell Multimixers.

3 Multimixers, ..., could make milkshakes in seconds.

4 That same year Ray visited a busy hamburger restaurant in California, ...

5 The restaurant, ..., served people amazingly quickly.

6 Ray introduced himself to the owners, ...

7 He suggested that they open more restaurants, ...

8 The first McDonald's, ..., was opened in Des Plaines, Illinois, in 1955.

a) He was an American salesman.
b) It was all the money he had.
c) They were large machines.
d) It used eight Multimixers at one time.
e) It was owned by Dick and Mac McDonald.
f) They turned out to be brothers.
g) He offered to run them.
h) It is now a museum and shows the history of McDonald's.

5 Open cloze

Read the text and think of the word that best fits each space. Use only one word in each space. There is an example at the beginning (0).

A HEALTHY DIET?

My grandfather, (0) ...*who*...... is in his seventies, adores junk food. My sister, (1) .... diet consists of little more than lettuce and yoghurt, is shocked by this. She thinks grandfather should eat things (2) .... are good for him, like lean meat and vegetables. 'The sort of diet (3) .... live on will make you ill!', she warns (4) .... But my grandfather isn't worried. He says people only need to worry (5) .... their diet if they aren't getting enough exercise. I think he's right. Think (6) .... office workers, for example. Many (7) .... them lead stressful lives and so they often eat for comfort. They have (8) .... sit at their desks for hours, (9) .... means they get very little exercise. It is hardly surprising (10) .... some get fat and end up suffering from heart disease.

Vocabulary ▶ CB p.61

1 Countable nouns

Put the words below under the correct heading. Write the table in your notebook.

Countable	Uncountable	Both

money   fruit   information   advice
loaf   time   energy   bottle   people
piece   meal   shopping   food   sugar
cheese   coffee

2 Which quantifier?

Fill in the gaps with a suitable quantifier.

1 How .... cans of Coke do we need for the party?

2 There were only a .... people in the gym.

3 We've hardly got .... ice cream left.

4 I've got very .... money on me – could you lend me some?

5 A: Would you like .... coffee?
B: Yes, just a ...., please.

6 How .... money did you spend today?

7 Very .... students in my class have eaten Chinese food.

8 I eat very .... chocolate.

3 Find the mistake

Two sentences are correct. Tick them. <u>Underline</u> the mistake in the other sentences and write the sentences correctly in your notebook.

1 Would you like a bread or some cereal?

2 I haven't got many time so I won't have breakfast today.

3 There are quite a little people coming to the party.

4 There aren't much pasta left, I'm afraid.

5 How many pieces of cake have you cut?

6 I need to buy some foods but I haven't got much money.

7 Shall we have chickens for dinner?

8 How much fruit should we eat a day, do you think?

4 Word sets: food

Look at the puzzle below and find:

1 a citrus fruit that tastes very bitter/sour
2 a type of fruit that is often crisp
3 three types of dairy products
4 flat, round pieces of potato cooked in oil and sold in bags as a savoury snack
5 something you eat raw in salad
6 two types of food that are rich in protein
7 a drink that you buy in cans
8 a food item that can be fresh or stale.

L	I	A	O	D	C	H	E	E	S	E
B	B	P	R	A	R	O	G	R	O	W
U	E	P	A	R	E	L	E	M	O	N
T	E	L	N	N	A	A	I	C	F	Y
T	F	E	G	Y	M	S	U	C	E	U
E	L	E	T	T	U	C	E	O	G	R
R	C	R	I	S	P	S	R	K	D	S
P	A	B	R	E	A	D	M	E	S	Y
C	H	I	C	H	I	C	K	E	N	P

5 Word formation

Fill in the gaps with a word from the list in the correct form. Be careful of spelling changes!

fizz / oil / taste / hunger / thirst / health

1 Tom was really .... so he ate three portions of chips!
2 I like .... drinks, like lemonade.
3 You should eat lots of vegetables if you want to stay ....
4 I didn't eat my chips because they were too ....
5 The meal was so .... that I had to have a second helping!
6 I drank a whole bottle of lemonade because I was so ....

6 Choosing the right word

Underline the correct word in each pair.

1 Is that The Hard Rock Café? I'd like to *book / rent* a table for four, please.
2 Waiter! Can we have the *menu / card*, please?
3 What would you like for your main *course / plate*?
4 I'll have a burger and a large *piece / portion* of chips, please.
5 There *aren't / isn't* any pasta left.
6 How many *helpings / amounts* of ice cream have you eaten?
7 Can I have another *can / container* of Coke, please?
8 I think I'll have a *piece / lump* of that delicious apple pie.
9 Could you *pass / leave* me the sugar, please?
10 Waiter! We'd like to pay the *receipt / bill*.

7 Lexical cloze

Decide which answer A, B or C best fits each space. There is an example at the beginning (0).

0	A the	B a	C one

PLANET HOLLYWOOD

Are you planning (0) ..*B*.. special celebration – a birthday, maybe, or a school outing? If you are, why not (1) .... a table at Planet Hollywood? The food is great. Take a look at the (2) .... and you will be amazed how (3) .... dishes you can choose from. The starters are delicious. Then, for your main (4) ...., you can have meat, pasta or vegetarian food. The (5) .... are very generous so (6) .... of your guests will go hungry! While you eat, you will be surrounded by non-stop entertainment including video clips of the (7) .... blockbusters and movie previews. Planet Hollywood also has the largest collection of movie memorabilia (8) .... the world. All in all, a party at this venue is an event to remember!

1	A hire	B rent	C book
2	A menu	B list	C card
3	A much	B many	C few
4	A serving	B course	C plate
5	A amount	B plates	C portions
6	A none	B little	C many
7	A latest	B last	C next
8	A on	B at	C in

Writing: report ▶ CB pp.63–64

1 Formal language

Tick the formal sentence, a) or b).

1 a) We had an absolutely terrific time!
   b) We had a wonderful time.

2 a) The entertainment was rather disappointing.
   b) The entertainment was really, really awful.

3 a) The staff were useless.
   b) The staff were extremely unhelpful.

4 a) The prices were very reasonable.
   b) You wouldn't believe the prices!

5 a) I wouldn't recommend eating there.
   b) Don't eat there, whatever you do!

6 a) The facilities are tremendous.
   b) You'll go crazy when you see the facilities.

7 a) Believe me, I had a great evening – it was the best!
   b) I had a very pleasant evening.

8 a) I can thoroughly recommend the band.
   b) The band was the tops!

2 Correct a sample answer

Read the writing task on p.63 of your Coursebook. Then look at the report that one student wrote and follow the instructions below.

1 The student has made three mistakes in style. Find them, underline them then write the sentences out more formally.

2 The student has not set out his report correctly. Write it out again in your notebook, dividing it into sections and adding headings where appropriate.

> *Dear Sir*
>
> *Here is my report on the new restaurant, 'The Stable'.*
>
> *'The Stable' is situated in the city centre. It's just across the road from the railway station so it's easy to get to. It's open five days a week, Tuesday to Saturday, from 7 p.m. to 1 a.m. The atmosphere is really, really fabulous! There's music every night and a live band on Fridays and Saturdays. On summer evenings, you can sit outside in the garden. You won't believe how good the food is! The menu offers a huge variety of meat and pasta dishes. There are loads and loads of vegetarian dishes too. Prices are extremely reasonable so young people can easily afford to eat here. To sum up, I would definitely recommend 'The Stable'. It offers delicious food, a lively atmosphere and it is not too expensive. I think it is an ideal place for students to go.*
>
> *Yours,*
>
> *Gary Brown*

3 Writing task

A group of young foreign tourists is coming to your town. You have been asked to write a report on a local amusement park, describing what people can do there and whether it's suitable for teenagers. Write your report in 120–180 words.

Remember to:

- divide your report into sections.
- use clear headings.
- check the style and format of your work.

8 House and home

Speaking ▶ CB p.65

▌Word sets: places to live

Fill in the gaps with a word from the list.

bungalow / block / fence / hedge / outskirts / cottage

1 There are no stairs in a ....

2 I live on the .... of the city, not in the centre.

3 In England, most people put up a .... round their back gardens.

4 For the summer, why not rent a pretty little .... in the country?

5 People who live in a .... of flats need to get on together.

6 Ken planted a .... at the back of his garden and he cuts it every month in summer.

▌Describing a photo

> ▶▶ *speaking strategy*
>
> When you compare photos and are asked to say which you prefer, try to give at least two reasons for your preferences. ◀◀

Look at the photos. <u>Underline</u> the correct option in each pair.

The first picture (1) *shows / is showing* a house. It's probably in the suburbs of a town. It's a detached house and (2) *is looking / looks* quite big. In the other photo, you (3) *can / could* see a flat. It's in a big block – I think it's called a skyscraper – in the centre of a city. There (4) *is / are* a man in the flat. He (5) *leans / is leaning* over the balcony. He (6) *is seeming / seems* to be holding something.

I think a flat like this (7) *has / is having* a lot of disadvantages. There (8) *isn't / aren't* much space, for example, and children (9) *aren't having / don't have* anywhere to play. It's very noisy too. A house (10) *is having / has* a lot of advantages for me. There (11) *is / are* much more room and it's much quieter too. Another advantage in a house is that you have a garden to relax in. I (12) *would / will* definitely prefer to live in a house.

Reading ▶ CB pp.66–67

1 Definitions

Replace the words in *italics* with an appropriate word from the list.

chill out / mean a lot / inspire / reflects / neat / hectic / weird / piles

Jason

1 Latin rock music helped to *give me ideas for* the look of my room. ....

2 My friends think my room is nice but others probably think it's a bit *strange*. ....

Simon

3 I leave my papers in *heaps, one on top of the other*, on the floor. ....

4 The bits and pieces I collected in Africa *are important* to me but not to anyone else. ....

5 My room is a safe place away from the *busy* life of the university. ....

Brian

6 I'm reasonably *tidy* but my mum always tidies my room. ....

Mohammed

7 Mohammed's room *shows* his interest in astronomy. ....

8 He thinks his room is a great place to *relax* after school. ....

2 Adjectives + prepositions

Fill in the gaps with an adjective from the list.
The prepositions are in *italics*, to help you.

crazy / terrible / keen / shocked / proud / happy

1 Sam's .... *about*
Manchester United – he's got
photos of David Beckham all
over his bedroom walls.

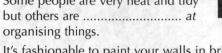

2 I decorated my room all by myself
so I feel quite .... *of* it.

3 Richard's not very ....
with his room because it's very small.

4 Some people are very neat and tidy
but others are .... *at*
organising things.

5 It's fashionable to paint your walls in bright colours but
I'm not .... *on* the idea.

6 Visitors are sometimes .... *by* the posters
students put on their walls.

3 Opposites

**1 Match an adjective from Column A with a word of
opposite meaning from Column B.**

A	B
1 fascinated	a) dangerous
2 hectic / very busy	b) bored / uninterested
3 ordinary / normal	c) messy
4 safe	d) peaceful / quiet
5 tidy	e) unimportant
6 essential	f) weird / strange

2 Now fill in the gaps with an appropriate word.

1 I can't find anything in my bedroom because it's so
....

2 We can manage without gas in the cottage but it's
.... that we have clean water.

3 Life in the countryside is very quiet and
....

4 It's .... to leave bottles of chemicals in the
kitchen without labelling them.

5 Mohammed is .... by astronomy so he's
painted stars on his ceiling.

6 There's a river near the house but it's not ....
to swim there because the water is polluted.

Grammar ▶ CB p.68, grammar file 12

1 *wish / if only* + past simple or *would*?

<u>Underline</u> the correct option in each pair.

1 Most teenagers wish they *had / would have* more
freedom.

2 Clare wishes she *didn't / wouldn't* have to live at home
any more.

3 If only my flatmates *were / would be* here now!

4 I wish you *switched / would switch* off the TV.

5 A lot of people wish they *were / would be* millionaires.

6 I wish I *would / could* afford my own flat.

7 Bob wishes his parents *would let / let* him get a dog.

8 I wish the sun *was / would be* shining!

9 If only our flat *had / would have* air conditioning!

10 Sometimes I wish I *were / would be* alone on a
desert island!

2 *wish*

Tick the correct option, a) or b).

1 I can't concentrate.
   a) I wish you stopped making such a noise.
   b) I wish you would stop making such a noise.

2 You live so far away!
   a) I wish you lived nearer.
   b) I wish you would live nearer.

3 Our flat is too small.
   a) I wish it were bigger.
   b) I wish it would be bigger.

4 I can't play the guitar.
   a) I wish someone taught me.
   b) I wish someone would teach me.

5 I'm at school.
   a) I wish I were on holiday.
   b) I wish I would be on holiday.

6 We love your garden.
   a) We wish we had your garden.
   b) We wish we would have your garden.

7 We can't afford a swimming pool.
   a) If only we were winning the lottery.
   b) If only we could win the lottery.

8 Roy's dreaming again!
   a) I wish he would concentrate.
   b) I wish he concentrated.

3 Verb forms

Fill in the gaps with the correct form of the verb in brackets.

1 I wish my parents .... (let) me get a flat with my friends.
2 Do you ever wish you .... (live) abroad?
3 A lot of teenage boys wish they .... (have) motorbikes or sports cars.
4 We'd enjoy this barbecue more if only it .... (stop) raining.
5 Don't you wish you .... (lie) on the beach at this moment instead of studying?
6 I wish that man .... (stop) staring at me!
7 I'm bored. If only my girlfriend .... (ring) me!
8 I wish you .... (not/interrupt) me. I'm trying to concentrate.

4 Captions

Look at the pictures. Use the prompts to make sentences.

1 wish/you/stop playing/guitar/so loud
....

2 wish/we/have/house/like Peter's
....

3 wish/the bus/come soon
....

4 If only/go/on holiday/next week
....

5 wish/speak English/more fluently
....

6 If only/not live/in the city
....

5 Error correction

Look carefully at each line. Three lines are correct. Tick them. The other lines each have one word which should not be there. <u>Underline</u> it. There are two examples at the beginning (0 and 00).

HOUSES OF THE FUTURE

  0   Do you like housework or, like most people, do you <u>are</u> wish
00   that someone else would do it all for you? Maybe you wish ✔
  1   that you would had a robot to tidy your bedroom? Your dream
  2   could come true a lot sooner than you were think! In less than
  3   25 years from now, experts predict that robot cleaners will be as
  4   common as washing machines they are today. And that's not all.
  5   Do you ever be wish that your bedroom was bigger? No problem!
  6   Future houses will have moveable walls so you'll be able to make
  7   a room any size you could like. Have you got noisy neighbours?
  8   Do you wish you could move it somewhere quieter? Don't worry!
  9   Future homes will be completely soundproof. You won't even have
10   know your neighbours exist!

Vocabulary ▶ CB p.69

1 *make* or *do*?

Four sentences are correct. Tick them. <u>Underline</u> the mistakes in the other sentences and correct them.

1 I hate making the housework! ....
2 Did you do your bed this morning? ....
3 I quite like doing the gardening. ....
4 Don't interrupt me. I'm making my homework. ....
5 I don't know how to make a cake. ....
6 Will you make the washing up tonight? ....
7 I've got no money so I can't do the shopping. ....
8 Don't do a noise or you'll wake the baby. ....
9 I wish you'd do an effort and help me with the cleaning! ....
10 Shall I make us a coffee? ....

Phrasal verbs

Fill in the gaps with a verb from the list. The particles are in *italics* to help you.

pull / put / tidy / take / done / wash / put / put

1 A British student is visiting my school for a week and we've offered to .... him *up*.
2 Before we can decorate my room, I'll have to .... *down* all my posters.
3 I always have to .... *up* after dinner.
4 This room's a mess so I'd better .... *up*.
5 I wish my sister would .... *away* her things when she's finished with them!
6 If you don't .... *up* any posters on the walls, the room will look quite bare.
7 The council is going to .... *down* the cinema and build new houses on the site.
8 The cottage was in very bad condition but the new owners have .... it *up* beautifully.

3 Choosing the right word

Look at the picture. Then <u>underline</u> the correct word in each pair.

1 The *ceiling / roof* is decorated with stars.
2 There's a *sink / washbasin* in the corner of the room.
3 The *ground / floor* is covered with magazines.
4 There are three *pillows / cushions* on the chair.
5 There's a suit hanging on the door of the *wardrobe / chest of drawers*.
6 There are some ornaments on the *shelf / counter*.

4 Word formation

1 Read the text below and <u>underline</u> which type of word is missing from the options given in brackets.

HOME ALONE

Stella and Fiona Simpson live on a deserted island off the coast of Britain. Apart from friends who come to visit, they are **(0)** .*completely*............ (*noun / <u>adverb</u>*) alone. They saw the island when they were on holiday and they **(1)** .... (*adverb / noun*) fell in love with it. When the only house on the island came up for sale, they decided to buy it. They gave up their well-paid jobs in London and moved. Their friends were **(2)** .... (*adjective / adverb*) at what they were doing but **(3)** ...., (*adjective / adverb*) the sisters have never regretted their decision. 'Since our **(4)** .... (*adjective / noun*) here, we haven't had one day's **(5)** .... (*adverb / noun*),' they told me. 'And it's so **(6)** .... (*adjective / adverb*)! London used to be very **(7)** ....' (*adjective / adverb*). The sisters are incredibly **(8)** .... (*adjective / adverb*). They repair the house themselves and grow their own food. Now in their eighties, they have no intention of leaving their 'dream' island.

2 Now fill in the missing words. Use the word in CAPITALS to form a noun, adjective or adverb that fits in the gap. Be careful! One gap needs a negative form. There is an example at the beginning (0).

0 COMPLETE   3 LUCK   6 PEACE
1 IMMEDIATE 4 ARRIVE   7 NOISE
2 AMAZE   5 ILL   8 DEPEND

Writing: article ▶ CB pp.71–72

1 Introductions and conclusions

1 Here are two introductions which two students wrote to start an article entitled 'My favourite meeting place'. Which of the introductions:

1 is too short? ....
2 is well-developed? ....
3 is lively and imaginative? ....
4 is a bit boring? ....
5 appeals to the reader's imagination? ....

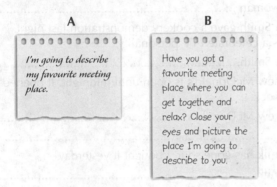

A

I'm going to describe my favourite meeting place.

B

Have you got a favourite meeting place where you can get together and relax? Close your eyes and picture the place I'm going to describe to you.

2 Now look at the two conclusions the students wrote.

Which of them:

1 rounds off the article in an interesting way? ....
2 would leave the reader feeling disappointed because it's short and rather boring? ....

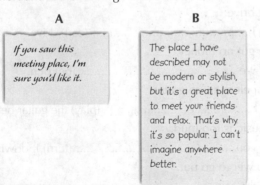

A

If you saw this meeting place, I'm sure you'd like it.

B

The place I have described may not be modern or stylish, but it's a great place to meet your friends and relax. That's why it's so popular. I can't imagine anywhere better.

2 Correct a sample answer

Read the writing task on p.71 of your Coursebook. Then look at the article that one student wrote and follow the instructions below.

1 The student should have divided her article into four paragraphs. Mark where you think each new paragraph could begin.
2 Rewrite the conclusion.
3 Correct the <u>underlined</u> mistakes in the article.

My favourite room

Imagine your favourite room. Is it modern or old, tidy or messy? The room I like most is in my <u>friends</u> house. My <u>friends</u> parents are farmers. Their house is <u>quiet</u> old – about 200 years, in fact. I like all the house but the living room <u>it's</u> my favourite. This room is best in winter because it's so warm and cosy. <u>It's</u> a big fireplace at one end. Around it, there are lots of old armchairs with bright covers. The chairs are so big <u>than</u> you can curl up and sleep <u>on</u> them. The room is really nice in summer, too. There's a door that goes <u>in</u> the garden and when the weather <u>will be</u> hot, it's always open. There are always lots of flowers in the room so it looks pretty and it <u>smell</u> nice as well. The living room walls are old and the ceiling is very low. You can often bang <u>the</u> head! There are old photos on the walls and piles of books everywhere. This room is never very tidy but <u>anybody</u> worries about that! If you saw this room, I'm sure you'd like it.

3 Writing task

You see this advertisement in a local paper.

WOULD YOU LIKE TO SEE YOUR ARTICLE IN PRINT?

We need articles for the weekly 'Reader's corner' page of our newspaper. Each successful writer will get their name in print and earn a substantial sum of money!

In this week's article, you should describe your favourite hotel.

Write your article in between 120–180 words.

Remember to:

- set your article out in paragraphs and to give it an interesting title.
- include a lively introduction and conclusion as your article must appeal to your readers.

Progress check 2

Grammar

1 Future tenses

Underline the correct option in each pair.

1 Tom: *We'll have / We're having* a party next Saturday. Can you come?

Clare: Sorry but *I'm going / I'll go* away next weekend. What a shame!

2 Mrs Lake: *I'm going to miss / I'm missing* you while *you're / you'll be* away.

Jon: Don't worry. I'll call you as soon as I *will get / get* to the hotel.

3 Paul: Listen, is that the doorbell?

Sue: Yes! *I'm going to go / I'll go* and see who it is.

4 Anne: *Will you do / Are you doing* anything special tonight?

Pete: Not really. I think *I'm just watching / I'll just watch* TV.

5 Jane: *Shall we play / Are we playing* a game of tennis?

Simon: No way! Look at the clouds. It *will / is going to* rain!

6 Ben: Hey, Jessica. *Will you dance / Are you dancing* with me?

Jessica: Yes, of course I *am / will*.

2 Conditionals

Fill in the gaps using the correct form of the verb in brackets.

1 Unless you .... (study) hard, you .... (fail) your test.

2 If I .... (be) you, I .... (get) some new trainers.

3 In Europe, if someone .... (shake) their head, they .... (mean) 'no'.

4 If you .... (get) the chance, please send me a postcard.

5 It's a shame I haven't got a mobile phone – I .... (ring) Jason if I .... (have).

6 If you .... (leave) that ice cream in the sun, it'll melt.

7 What a pity I forgot my address book. If I .... (know) his address, I .... (can /send) him a card.

8 If you .... (switch on) the computer, you may find an e-mail waiting for you.

3 Relative clauses

Combine the sentences. Add commas and relative pronouns where necessary.

1 Some people organised the barbecue. They were great fun.
The people ....

2 I know someone. His father is a well-known chef.
I know someone ....

3 I ate a meal last night. It was fantastic.
The meal ....

4 I spoke to a woman. She's written a new cookbook.
The woman ....

5 Delia Smith gave a cookery demonstration last night. She is a celebrated TV personality.
Delia Smith, ...

6 The new McDonald's is open until midnight. It opened last week.
The new McDonald's, ...
....

7 The milk has gone sour. I bought it yesterday.
The milk ....

8 The pizza place was empty. I ate in it.
The pizza place ....

4 Wishes

Fill in the gaps using the verb in brackets. You may need to add other words.

1 I can't drive.
I wish I .... (can) drive.

2 We've got no money.
I wish we .... (be) rich.

3 I'm hopeless at the guitar.
I wish I .... (play) the guitar better.

4 The music is too loud.
I wish you .... (turn) it down.

5 It's too wet to go out.
I wish the rain .... (stop).

6 It's a long way to your house.
I wish you .... (be) nearer.

44

Vocabulary

5 Choosing the right word

<u>Underline</u> the correct word in each pair.

1 The car broke down on the *road*/*way* to the airport.
2 You should exercise if you want to stay *fine*/*healthy*.
3 Jane's dad cooked us a fantastic *plate*/*meal*.
4 I have to be careful of my diet *because*/*although* I'm diabetic.
5 The waiter didn't *give*/*make* me a chance to explain.
6 You shouldn't have drunk *some*/*all* the milk in the fridge.
7 How *much*/*many* exercise did you get yesterday?
8 I eat *lots of*/*several* fruit every day.
9 Would you like *a little*/*a few* grapes?
10 I take *much*/*very little* sugar in my tea.

6 Word formation

1 Complete the table.

Noun	Adjective	Negative adjective	Positive adverb
care	1	2	3 ....
4	5	6	obediently
7	fit	8	xxx
fortune	9	10	11 ....
success	12	13	14 ....
15	16	17	patiently
18	probable	19	20 ....
hope	21	22	23 ....
24	25	unhappy	26 ....
profession	27	28	29 ....

2 Use the word in CAPITALS at the end of each sentence to form a new word that fits in the gap.

1 Jim's a good teacher because he has lots of .... PATIENT
2 Unfortunately, their attempt to reach the North Pole was .... SUCCESS
3 David Beckham is a .... footballer. PROFESSION
4 The pupil was punished because she was .... OBEY

5 Students who study hard will .... get good grades in the exam. PROBABLE
6 .... is very important if you want to excel at sport. FIT
7 She fell off her horse but .... she wasn't injured. FORTUNE
8 The judge fined the motorist £2,000 for driving .... CARE

7 Adjectives and adverbs

<u>Underline</u> the correct word in each pair.

1 The bride and groom look really *happy*/*happily*.
2 I'm *extreme*/*extremely* sorry.
3 We could *hard*/*hardly* hear the music.
4 He shouted *angry*/*angrily*.
5 I'm *absolutely*/*extremely* happy.
6 I felt *really*/*absolutely* scared.
7 The teacher was *rather*/*utterly* furious.
8 We were a *bit*/*absolutely* horrified.

8 Prepositions

Fill in the gaps with the correct preposition.

1 I had pasta .... lunch.
2 We go skiing .... winter.
3 I didn't go .... holiday last year.
4 We live .... the country.
5 I play football .... weekends.
6 The lesson is over .... last!
7 Do you know what's on .... the cinema?
8 My friends have gone .... a school trip.

9 Phrasal verbs

Fill in the gaps with a verb from the list. You will need to use some words more than once.

put / take / tidy / wash

1 You should .... *up* your bedroom!
2 They are going to .... *up* a new housing estate on the empty land.
3 I always .... *up* after dinner.
4 .... *away* your things and get ready for dinner.
5 I'll have to .... *down* all my pictures because my room is going to be decorated.
6 We offered to .... *up* some of the visitors in our house.

9 Music

Speaking ▶ CB p.75

1 Word sets: musical categories

1 Look at the words in the box. Put them under the correct heading. Write the table in your notebook.

People	Instruments	Equipment	Types of music
lead singer			

jazz   electric guitar   microphone   rap   drums   orchestra
salsa   audience   lead singer   classical   band   group
loudspeaker   keyboards   pop   violinist

2 Fill in the gaps with an appropriate word.

1 A person who plays records at a disco is called a ..*disc jockey*... .
2 A person who plays music is called a ....
3 A person who plays the drums is a ....
4 A person who plays the guitar is a ....
5 A person who writes music (like Beethoven) is a ....
6 A person who leads an orchestra is a ....
7 A person who follows a rock group and collects their photos and autographs is called a ....
8 A person who sings solo is a ....

2 Preferences

Look at the two photos. Then fill in the gaps with a correct word from the list. You will not need to use all of the words.

whereas / young / much / fun / prefer / keen / kind / stage / in / there / events / because / probably / rather

These photos show very different types of events. The people (1) .... the first photo are at some (2) .... of music festival. They're standing in front of a (3) .... and watching the musicians. They all look quite (4) .... – there are no older people there. I think it's probably a hot day (5) .... some people are wearing sun hats or scarves on their heads.

The other photo is (6) .... of a disco. The people here are (7) .... more energetic than the people at the music festival. I can see a DJ at the front. (8) .... are lots of young people dancing in the room.

I think I'd much (9) .... to go to a music festival than a disco. I'm not very (10) .... on discos at all, actually. Live performances are far more exciting. And of course, discos only last a few hours, (11) .... festivals sometimes go on for days. You can have more (12) .... outdoors, as well.

Reading ▶ CB pp.76–77

1 Summarising

The following sentences summarise how to create a hit album. Number them in the correct order. Check your answers by looking at p.76 of the Coursebook.

☐ a) They make notes of any changes to the lyrics of a new song.
☐ b) The completed song goes on sale in the shops.
☐ c) They record more instruments and add them to the recording on the hard disc.
☐ d) a1 arrive at the studio.
☐ e) They save the vocals onto a computer disc.
☐ f) The producer puts together the final, completed song.
☐ g) They record their voices.
☐ h) The producer goes into the control room and gets the recording console ready.

2 Prepositions

Fill in the gaps with the correct preposition from the list.

by / at / for / in / on / onto / through / at

1 The band spent the day .... the recording studio.

2 They are appearing .... stage tonight.

3 The band arrive .... work very early in the morning.

4 They are following .... the footsteps of many other famous groups.

5 They know the words to all their songs .... heart.

6 When they record songs, they save them .... a computer.

7 You can listen to that song .... my headphones if you like.

8 It's not .... all easy to become a successful pop group.

Grammar ▶ CB p.78, grammar file 14

1 Sentence completion

Tick the correct option, a) or b).

1 Do you know …
   a) what time does the show finish?
   b) what time the show finishes?

2 Can anybody tell me …
   a) how this video machine works?
   b) how does work this video machine?

3 I'd like to know …
   a) how much are the drinks.
   b) how much the drinks are.

4 Could you tell me if …
   a) I can get tickets here?
   b) can I get tickets here?

5 Could you tell me …
   a) how to get to the stage door?
   b) how do I get to the stage door?

6 Do you know whether Boyzone …
   a) are appearing here tonight?
   b) are they appearing here tonight?

7 Have you got any idea …
   a) where do we go to get autographs?
   b) where we go to get autographs?

2 Indirect questions

Rewrite these questions, beginning *Do you know* …?

1 Is Eric Clapton a famous guitarist?
   Do you know ...*if Eric Clapton is a famous guitarist*.................?

2 Does Madonna come from the USA?
   Do you know ....?

3 Did Paul McCartney play with The Beatles?
   ....?

4 Are Boyzone still making records?
   ....?

5 Has Celine Dion released a new CD?
   ....?

6 Was Mick Jagger a drummer with The Rolling Stones?
   ....?

7 Is John Lennon still alive?
   ....?

8 Can Eminem play the guitar?
   ....?

3 Prompted sentences

Use the prompts to complete the sentences. Make any changes necessary. Be careful with tenses.

1 Do you know ...*what time the concert starts tonight*.................?
   (what time / concert / start / tonight)

2 You know the band a1? Have you any idea ....
   ....? (who / lead singer / be)

3 Could you tell me ....
   ....? (where / I / able / get / tickets / for next week's show)

4 I wonder if you could tell me ....
   .... (where / Hearsay / play / next week)

5 Excuse me. Can you tell me ....
   ....? (when / last bus / leave / tonight)

6 I'd like to know ....
   .... (whether / Martine McCutcheon / sing / tonight)

7 Can you remind me ....
   ....? (what time / rehearsals / start / tomorrow)

8 You know the singer Robbie Williams? Can you tell me
   ....? (where / come / from)

9 Excuse me. Do you know whether ....
   ....? (this train / go / city centre)

10 Have you any idea if ....?
   (a1 / arrive / yet)

4 Open cloze

Read the text and think of the word that best fits each space. Use only one word in each space. There is an example at the beginning (0).

Dear John,

I heard you were organising **(0)** ....*a*.... rock festival in town this summer and I was wondering if you **(1)** .... tell me a bit more about it.

Do you know **(2)** .... bands are going to play? It would be great **(3)** .... a boy band like a1 would agree to come! Can you also **(4)** .... me where the festival will be held? Will it be outdoors, like last year? I'd also like **(5)** .... know how much the tickets cost. The last time we had a rock festival, it **(6)** .... cheaper for young people under 18. Do you think the same discounts **(7)** .... be available this summer?

Finally, I'd like to **(8)** .... whether you need volunteers to help with the festival. Please **(9)** .... me know if I can help in any way.

I look forward to hearing **(10)** .... you,

Chris

5 Transformations

Complete the second sentence so that it has a similar meaning to the first sentence, using the word given. Do not change the word given. Use between two and five words.

1 Where can I buy a1's new single? **know**

Do you .... a1's new single?

2 How old is Eminem? **idea**

Have you any ....?

3 What time does the show start tonight? **starts**

I wonder if you could tell me .... tonight.

4 Am I right or not? **whether**

Can you tell me .... or not?

5 Where can I get a drink, please? **know**

I'd like to .... a drink, please.

6 Could you help me? **if**

I wonder .... me.

7 Did I leave my wallet here? **whether**

Could you tell me .... here?

8 What time does the box office open in the morning? **when**

I'd like to know .... in the morning.

Vocabulary ▶ CB p.79

1 Word sets: music

Fill in the gaps with the correct word from the list.

beat / headphones / heart / lyrics / tune / voice

1 The song has a .... you can dance to.

2 I can't remember the words of *Yesterday*, but I can hum the ....

3 I know the words of most of Whitney Houston's songs by ....

4 If I wear ...., I can listen to my Walkman without disturbing anyone else.

5 Andrew Lloyd Webber composed the music for *Cats* and Tim Rice wrote the ....

6 I love listening to Britney Spears – she's got a really original ....

2 At a concert

Label the picture using the words in the box.

| stage | loudspeakers | microphone |
| guitarist | singer / soloist | drummer |

3 Verbs that show appreciation

Fill in the gaps with a verb from the list.

cry / cheered / clap / chant / boo / tap

1 When Eminem finally appeared, the crowd
....

2 Come on everybody, ... your hands together!

3 The crowd started to .... angrily when they realised the singer hadn't turned up.

4 The soundtrack to *Love Story* is so sad – it always makes me ....!

5 The crowd started to .... Madonna's name, over and over again.

6 Everyone began to .... their feet to the beat.

4 Choosing the right word

Underline the correct word in each pair.

1 Can you remember the *harmony / soundtrack* to the last James Bond film?

2 There was a long *row / queue* outside the box office.

3 Singers don't always write their own *lyrics / vocals*.

4 The songs Paul McCartney wrote *achieved / made* him a millionaire.

5 The singers in the musical were dressed in amazing *costumes / robes*.

6 The singer, Björk, is appearing live on *platform / stage* tonight.

7 The Corrs are going *in / on* tour again soon.

8 I belong to Celine Dion's fan *club / group*.

5 Phrasal verbs

Fill in the gaps with a verb from the list. The particles are in *italics*, to help you.

let / turn / put / bring / joined / split

1 The show should have begun at 8 p.m. but the band didn't .... *up* until 10!

2 Some members of Boyzone want solo careers, so the band will probably .... *up* soon.

3 The lead singer's ill so the organisers have .... *off* the show until next week.

4 They're going to .... *out* the soundtrack of the film on CD soon.

5 Some people started clapping and soon the whole audience .... *in*.

6 Stella promised to come to the show with me but she .... me *down* at the last minute.

6 Lexical cloze

Read the text and decide which answer A, B or C best fits each space. There is an example at the beginning (0).

| 0 | A less | B fewer | C little |

MADONNA

Nowadays, **(0)** ..*B*... bands go on tour than in the past. Audiences have got smaller because **(1)** .... cost so much these days. This is not true for Madonna, **(2)** .... Tickets for her latest tour **(3)** .... out within hours. All round the country, fans formed long **(4)** .... outside box offices, desperate to see their idol live on **(5)** ....

Madonna is one of the world's most successful solo artists. Her music includes pop, R&B and hip hop. She **(6)** .... out her first number 1 single, *Like a Virgin*, back in 1984. Other **(7)** .... singles, like *Material Girl* and *Nothing Really Matters,* have **(8)** .... her a millionaire. In 1996, she recorded the **(9)** .... for the movie *Evita* in which she also played the title role. Her singing **(10)** .... is strong and rich. Madonna is famous for her extravagant **(11)** .... and her dancing. She married actor Sean Penn in 1985 but they **(12)** .... up in 1988. She is now married to UK film director Guy Ritchie and has two children.

1	A admissions	B tickets	C entrances
2	A however	B although	C but
3	A gave	B made	C sold
4	A rows	B queues	C files
5	A platform	B place	C stage
6	A brought	B gave	C took
7	A chart	B hit	C song
8	A done	B achieved	C made
9	A soundtrack	B tune	C beat
10	A lyric	B vocal	C voice
11	A robes	B cloths	C costumes
12	A separated	B split	C divorced

Writing: formal transactional letter

▶ CB pp.81–82

Expanding notes

You saw an advertisement for a rock concert and made some notes. You are preparing to write to the organisers with questions about the concert. Expand the notes into indirect questions, starting with the words given.

1 when does rock concert begin?

I wonder ....*if you could tell me what time the rock concert begins* .

2 how to get there?

Could you ....?

3 which bands to play?

I'd like to know ....

4 what time does concert start?

Can you tell me ....?

5 how much tickets cost?

I'd be grateful if you could tell me ....

Correct a sample answer

Read the writing task on p.81 of your Coursebook. Then look at the letter that one student wrote and follow the instructions below.

1 The student made mistakes when expanding notes into sentences. Find the mistakes and correct them.

2 The student would have sounded more polite if he had used indirect questions. Write the letter out again in your notebook, changing all the questions from direct to indirect questions.

> Dear sir,
> I've just seen your advertisement for the festival in today's issue of 'Rock' magazine. Could you answer a few questions?
> First, is accommodation nearby? I'm a student so I haven't got much money. Maybe I can camp? Is there a campsite?
> Second, which bands playing? I'm keen on heavy rock and rap music so I hope there will be some music like that.
> Finally, could you tell me if discounts for students? Also, do I need to book long time in advance?
> I look forward to hearing from you.
> Yours faithfully,

3 Writing task

You saw this advertisement in a music magazine. Read the advertisement and the notes you made next to it. Then write to the Production Manager, saying you are interested in taking part and asking for more information.

Write a letter of 120–180 words in an appropriate style.

Remember to:

- read the exam task carefully. Make sure you include all the points you are asked for.
- set out your text as a letter with the correct beginning and ending. Check who is going to read the letter and make sure you use an appropriate style.
- expand notes into full sentences. Use the correct punctuation.
- use indirect questions where appropriate so that you sound polite.

10 Success

Speaking ▶ CB p.83

Stating opinions

> ▶▶ *speaking strategy*
>
> When you state an opinion, make sure you give reasons. Encourage your partner to speak by asking for his/her opinions. Try not to interrupt when he/she is speaking. ◀◀

Two students are discussing which of the factors in the box could be important if you want to be a famous film actor. Read their conversation. Then fill in the gaps with a suitable word or phrase.

- acting talent   • looks
- knowing people who can help you
- intelligence   • health
- personality

A: Right. We've got to say which of these is most important. What (1) .... about intelligence?

B: Well, I think (2) .... very important because lots of actors aren't very bright.

A: Yes, you're (3) ....

B: What (4) .... health? I don't think it's very important, do you?

A: Oh, I think it (5) ....! Film actors have to work long hours in front of the cameras.

B: OK, maybe it helps – but it's not that (6) ....

A: Maybe not. I think personality is very important, don't (7) ....?

B: Yes, but I think looks are more important, because that's what audiences see on screen.

A: (8) .... true.

B: What about knowing people who can help you? That's not important, is it?

A: Oh, don't you think (9) ....? I think it is! I think actors need all the help they can get, especially in the beginning!

B: That's a good point. Now, what about acting talent?

A: I think that's definitely the most important, don't you?

B: Yes, I do.

A: OK, do we both (10) .... about the factors we think are important? Let's check again. …

Reading ▶ CB pp.84–85

1 Definitions

1 Complete the definitions with words from the list.

achievement / environment / genius / inspiration / talent / theory

1 .... (n.) natural ability

2 .... (n.) explanation that is not yet proved

3 .... (n.) person with a very high level of intelligence

4 .... (n.) success in something you have worked hard for

5 .... (n.) surroundings

6 .... (n.) something that gives you the idea to do something

2 Replace the words in *italics* with an appropriate word from the list.

exceptionally / composing / bright / remarkable / neglected / lack the drive / persistence / claims

1 Dineshi is very *intelligent*. ....

2 Children like Dineshi seem *unbelievably* intelligent. ....

3 According to Professor Howe, these children's success is due to practice, *determination* and a suitable environment. ....

4 Mozart was already *writing* music at the age of 5. ....

5 Professor Howe *says* that Mozart didn't start to write great music until he was 21. ....

6 In the early 1900s, people said Billy Sidis was the most *unusual* boy in the USA. ....

7 Billy's parents had *failed* to teach him important social skills. ....

8 Many people who have high IQs often *don't have the motivation* to succeed. ....

2 Words that go together

Fill in the gaps with the correct form of a verb from the list. Each word goes with the word(s) in *italics*.

achieve / suffer / go / try / give / compose

1 Mark's parents wanted him to be a genius but they .... *wrong* somewhere!

2 I want to .... *something great* before I'm old.

3 Mozart started to .... *music* when he was five years old.

4 Last week, the headmaster .... us a *lecture* on Einstein.

5 I .... *hard* but I still can't learn the piano!

6 The painter, Van Gogh, ... *a breakdown* while he was living in France.

Grammar ▶ CB p.86, grammar file 11

1 Third conditional

Combine the sentences using the third conditional.

1 Princess Diana loved Prince Charles. She married him.
If Princess Diana ......*hadn't loved*.................. Prince Charles, she ..*wouldn't have married*.......... him.

2 We didn't go to the film festival. We didn't see Julia Roberts.
We .... Julia Roberts if we .... to the film festival.

3 Marilyn Monroe was beautiful. Her photos appeared everywhere.
If Marilyn Monroe ...., her photos .... everywhere.

4 I didn't attend the lecture. I didn't hear the scientist, Stephen Hawking, talk about the cosmos.
I .... the scientist, Stephen Hawking, talk about the cosmos if I .... the lecture.

5 Kelly didn't pass the screen test. She didn't get a part in the play.
If Kelly .... the screen test, she .... a part in the play.

6 Joanne Rowling wrote the *Harry Potter* books. She became a millionaire.
Joanne Rowling .... a millionaire if she .... the *Harry Potter* books.

2 Find the mistake

Two of the sentences are correct. Tick them.
Underline the mistakes in the other sentences and correct them.

1 We wouldn't have got tickets for the concert if we wouldn't have queued all night. ....

2 If Bill Gates hadn't invented *Windows* software, he might not have became a millionaire. ....

3 You would have seen the Manchester United team if you went to the football stadium yesterday. ....

4 If my sister won the talent competition last week, she would probably have appeared on TV. ....

5 If President Kennedy hadn't gone to Dallas, Texas, a madman wouldn't have shot him. ....

6 Walt Disney might not have made cartoons if he wouldn't have been good at design. ....

7 Would anyone have heard of John Lennon if he hadn't been a member of The Beatles? ....

8 I would have joined a rock band if my parents would have let me. ....

3 *wish*

Look at the pictures and complete the captions. Use the words in brackets to help you.

1 I wish I ....*hadn't married you*...........! (marry)

2 I wish I ....! (camera)

3 I wish I ....! (miss)

4 I wish I ....! (petrol)

5 I wish I ....! (suit)

6 I wish I ....! (break)

4 Transformations

Complete the second sentence so that it has a similar meaning to the first, using the word given. Do not change the word given. Use between two and five words.

1 I'm sorry I didn't ask Madonna for her autograph. **wish**
I .... Madonna for her autograph.

2 We arrived late so we didn't see the President. **if**
We might have seen the President .... earlier.

3 Alice didn't go to the audition because she was ill. **would**
If Alice hadn't been ill, she .... the audition.

4 I'm sorry I missed Brad Pitt's latest film. **I**
I wish .... Brad Pitt's latest film.

5 The astronaut Yuri Gagarin became famous because he went to the moon. **have**
The astronaut Yuri Gagarin .... famous if he hadn't gone to the moon.

6 I'm sorry I didn't see the programme about Agatha Christie. **only**
If .... the programme about Agatha Christie.

7 Peter regrets going to Hollywood. **wishes**
Peter .... to Hollywood.

8 Sarah didn't win the lottery so she didn't get her photo in the paper. **had**
If Sarah had won the lottery, she .... her photo in the paper.

5 Open cloze

Read the text and think of the word that best fits each space. Use only one word in each space. There is an example at the beginning (0).

FAME!

Do you ever wish you **(0)** ...*could*............... change your life? Maybe you wish you **(1)** .... been born rich or that you **(2)** .... a top model or pop idol?

Wishes rarely come true but for Paul McCartney they did. Paul **(3)** .... a very ordinary boy, at school **(4)** .... the North of England, when fame called. In his free time, Paul played **(5)** .... guitar and sang. Then he met John Lennon. If the two boys **(6)** .... not got on together, nothing more would **(7)** .... happened. But they became great friends. They formed a band called The Beatles.

Maybe nobody would have heard of The Beatles **(8)** .... the boys hadn't started to write their own songs. These songs, like *Yesterday* and *Hey Jude*, made them famous worldwide. They went **(9)** .... tour and fans went crazy. In the end, life became so dangerous that they **(10)** .... to hide from the public. After only seven years, the group split up. If they hadn't **(11)** .... so popular, maybe they **(12)** .... have stayed together longer. This was not the end for Paul or John, however. Both became famous as solo artists. Meanwhile, Beatles music is still played all over the world.

Vocabulary ▶ CB p.87

1 Word formation

Fill in the gaps with the correct form of the word in CAPITALS. In this exercise, you will need an adjective or a noun.

1 These days, rock stars are amazingly .... on stage. ENERGY

2 Where did Agatha Christie get the .... for her crime books? INSPIRE

3 Most people are curious about the .... lives of the rich and famous. PERSON

4 .... is a problem for many famous people. LONELY

5 Stephen Hawking has been a very .... figure in the field of science. INFLUENCE

6 Henry will never get to the top because he lacks .... MOTIVE

7 Actress Kate Beckinsale arrived at the premiere looking very .... GLAMOUR

8 Top film directors like Steven Spielberg possess a great deal of .... CREATIVE

9 If you want to be .... in life, you need luck as well as talent. SUCCESS

10 Most children at the audition were not very talented but Tanya was really .... EXCEPTION

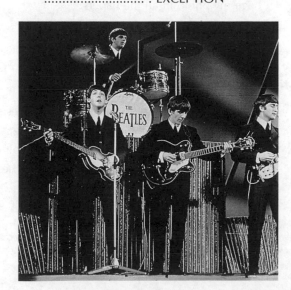

2 Opposites

1 Match a word from Column A with an opposite word from Column B.

A		B	
1	courageous	a)	clever
2	energetic	b)	cowardly
3	exceptional	c)	hopeless
4	famous	d)	intolerant
5	talented	e)	lazy
6	optimistic	f)	ordinary
7	stupid	g)	peaceful
8	tolerant	h)	pessimistic
9	violent	i)	unknown

2 Fill in the gaps using a word from the list above.

1 Carla is brilliant at Physics but I'm completely
....

2 Until Hollywood discovered him, Leonardo DiCaprio was
practically ....

3 Bill's instructor says he'll pass the driving test but Bill seems
rather .... about it.

4 Daniel works hard but Harry is really ....!
He sits in a chair all day, watching TV.

5 Ella came first in her exams – she's a really ....
girl.

6 My parents are very ....; they let me say and do
what I want.

7 The first astronaut to land on the moon was very
.... because he knew that what he was doing
was very dangerous.

8 I want to be a .... scientist when I'm older and
have my photo in all the papers.

3 Verb + preposition

Fill in the gaps with the correct preposition. The verb is in *italics* to help you.

1 The Queen *insisted* .... greeting all her guests personally.

2 The actress *accused* the producer .... lying.

3 Security guards *discouraged* fans .... climbing onto the stage.

4 The film *Gladiators succeeded* .... taking the most Oscars at
the film awards.

5 The Beatles *contributed* a great deal .... the development of
pop music.

6 Please *forgive* me .... damaging your video.

4 Word formation

Read the text and decide which answer A, B or C best fits each space. There is an example at the beginning (0).

0	**A** more	**B** most	**C** great

MOTHER TERESA

Mother Teresa is one of the **(0)** ...*B*.... influential
personalities of the twentieth century. However,
her life was **(1)** .... easy nor glamorous.
When she was young, she went to India **(2)** ....
a missionary. She became a **(3)** .... of English
in a secondary school. The school was in a nice
area but there were slums **(4)** .... Conditions
there were **(5)** .... terrible. She was **(6)** ....
by what she saw. She **(7)** .... on leaving her
comfortable convent and going to live **(8)** ....
the poor. At first her superiors tried to **(9)** ....
her from leaving the convent but in the end
they **(10)** .... to let her go.

Soon other people heard about her work and
came to help her. Although she had no money
herself, she **(11)** .... in building shelters for
the dying and schools for the poor. By the
1990s she had **(12)** .... famous and she was
eventually given the Nobel Prize for her service
to the poor.

1	**A** nor	**B** either	**C** neither
2	**A** as	**B** to	**C** like
3	**A** professor	**B** trainer	**C** teacher
4	**A** next	**B** nearby	**C** beside
5	**A** very	**B** absolutely	**C** awfully
6	**A** horrified	**B** depressing	**C** sad
7	**A** decided	**B** though	**C** insisted
8	**A** between	**B** among	**C** along
9	**A** persuade	**B** convince	**C** discourage
10	**A** agreed	**B** accepted	**C** allowed
11	**A** won	**B** succeeded	**C** managed
12	**A** became	**B** been	**C** become

Writing: story ▶ CB pp.89–90

1 Time expressions

> ┌ ! *tip* ─────────────────────
> Remember to use time expressions to sequence events
> in a story.

**Fill in the gaps with *at*, *in*, *after* or *afterwards*.
The time expressions are in *italics* to help you.**

1 Monika didn't feel very happy .... *the beginning* of the evening.

2 She hadn't wanted to come .... *the first place* because she didn't know anyone there.

3 She didn't talk to anyone .... *first*.

4 She sat in the corner for a long time but .... *the end* Bob asked her to dance.

5 They got on well and arranged to walk home together .... *the end* of the evening.

6 *The next day* they went to the cinema and, ..., they went for a coffee.

7 Monika was very happy because .... *last* she had a boyfriend of her own.

8 .... *a few days*, she took Bob to meet her parents.

2 Tenses

Fill in the gaps with the correct form of the verb in brackets.

I (1) .... (get) off the bus when a young man (2) .... (shout) out to me. He (3) .... (sit) on a bench near the bus station, drinking a Coke. When he (4) .... (saw) me, he (5) .... (jump) up and (6) .... (ask) me the time. We (7) .... (start) chatting and (8) .... (find out) that we (9) .... (live) in the same street. Imagine! We were neighbours but we (10) .... (never speak) to each other before! We (11) .... (stand) there talking when suddenly something really amazing (12) .... (happen).

3 Correct a sample answer

Read the writing task on p.89 of your Coursebook. Then look at the story one student wrote.

The student has:

1 made mistakes with time linkers, which the teacher has <u>underlined</u>.

2 made some punctuation mistakes.

Write the story out again correctly in your notebook.

> As soon as Peter read about the competition, he knew he had to take part It was a fancy dress competition and it would take place the following Saturday.
>
> <u>On the beginning</u> he didn't know what to wear. He thought about hiring a costume but it was too expensive. <u>At the end,</u> his grandmother made his costume he was going to be Robin Hood. When he put on the costume he looked very handsome. His uncle whose hobby was archery lent him a real bow.
>
> Saturday came and the judging began. Peter was nervous <u>in first</u> but he soon relaxed. He was sure he could win but he wanted the judge to notice him. What could he do. I know, he said. He took his bow and shot an arrow.
>
> It was lucky the arrow was plastic. The judge was shocked but there was no mark to show where the arrow hit him Peter was disqualified, of course. <u>On the end</u> the judge gave the prize to 'Cleopatra'. Peter has never taken part in a competition again.

4 Writing task

A magazine is asking readers to send in short stories. The stories must begin with the following words:

> *I will never forget the day . . .*

Write your story for the magazine in 120–180 words.

Remember to:

- brainstorm ideas. Ask yourself questions like:
  1 What is the first line of the story?
  2 What was special about 'the day'? Why will you never forget it?
  3 Who are the main characters in the story?
  4 How did the day begin?
  5 What were the main events of the day?
  6 How did the day end? How did you feel?
- use a range of past tenses to tell your story.
- check your work for spelling and punctuation mistakes.

11 Lifestyles

Speaking ▶ CB p.91

Describing pictures

Look at the two pictures. Then read the text and <u>underline</u> the correct option in each pair.

In the first picture (1) *they / there* are some young people. They're in class but they (2) *seem / look like* very relaxed. Nobody (3) *seems / looks* to be working, except for the boy on the left. Maybe he's just playing a game. I think it's probably break time or maybe lessons are finished for the day.

In the second picture, they are at school as well. They're sitting in a classroom, like the children in the first picture. But I (4) *get / am* the impression that the students are not very happy. The students (5) *seem to be / look as if* afraid of the teacher. He (6) *looks / looks as if* very strict. The boy in the corner (7) *looks as if / seems* he's in trouble. Maybe the teacher (8) *is punishing / punishes* him for something. I don't know why. It's difficult to say. I don't think I'd like to go to that school. I'd prefer (9) *to go / going* to the modern school. It (10) *seems / looks like* much nicer.

Reading ▶ CB pp.92–93

1 True or false?

Read these sentences and decide if they are true (T) or false (F). Check your answers by reading the text in your Coursebook pp.92–93.

1 Jimmy lives in the same place as his ancestors used to live. ...*T*...

2 In the past, the Inuit occasionally died from lack of food. ....

3 The Inuit no longer know how to make their own instruments. ....

4 In the past, the Inuit travelled everywhere on foot. ....

5 Now, Inuit children are not taught a great deal about their own traditions. ....

6 Jimmy has a good relationship with his grandmother. ....

7 Jimmy thinks the Inuit language may disappear in the future. ....

8 Jimmy is optimistic about the future. ....

2 Words that go together

1 Match a verb from Column A with a word from Column B.

A	B
1 attend	a) advice
2 feel	b) clothes
3 give	c) school
4 hunt	d) time
5 make	e) an effort
6 spend	f) a subject
7 study	g) animals
8 wear	h) left out

2 Then fill in the gaps with an appropriate word. Be careful of tenses!

1 Jimmy .... an American school.

2 He .... rather left out of his culture.

3 The elders are happy to .... advice to young people.

4 In the past, the Inuit .... animals like caribou.

5 Jimmy thinks people should .... an effort to hold on to their traditions.

6 In the old days, people .... more time travelling.

7 Jimmy .... American subjects at school.

8 He always .... American clothes.

3 Definitions

Replace the words in *italics* with an appropriate word from the list.

supposed to / gets in the way of / tribe / ancestors / up to everyone / starve

1 Nothing *prevents him from* going to basketball practice.

....

2 Jimmy still lives in the same area as his *family members who lived a long time before his grandparents*.

....

3 In bad weather, people would *die for lack of food*.

....

4 Young Inuits can learn traditional ways from the elders of their *group which has the same language, culture and traditions*. ....

5 Jimmy and his friends are *expected to* learn their own language at school. ....

6 Jimmy feels that it's *everyone's responsibility* to make things change. ....

Grammar ▶ CB p.94, grammar files 4, 7

1 Past habit

Match the sentence halves to make logical sentences.

A	B
1 I never	a) was busy.
2 My friends are	b) use to bite his nails?
3 Did you	c) usually walk to school with me.
4 My friend doesn't	d) often stay out all day when you were little?
5 Did Patrick	e) used to like swimming in the sea.
6 I didn't answer because I	f) usually wear jeans to school?
7 Would you	g) always making me laugh.
8 Does Clare	h) use to play 'doctors and nurses' when you were young?

2 *used to* or *would*?

<u>Underline</u> the correct option in each pair. Sometimes both options are possible.

1 When we were young, we *would often / often used to* go to the park.

2 My best friend *would / used to* be one of the naughtiest children in the school.

3 As a child, I *would / used to* be really scared of spiders.

4 My brother and I *would often / often used to* pretend to be aliens from another planet.

5 When I was little, I *would / used to* believe there were ghosts under the bed!

6 *Did you use to / Would you* know many nursery rhymes when you were young?

7 My grandmother *used to / would* be very beautiful when she was young.

8 I *never used to / would never* like school when I was younger.

3 Find the mistake

**Two sentences are correct. Tick them.
<u>Underline</u> the mistakes in the other sentences
and correct them.**

1 We use to go hunting when we lived in the
country. ....

2 I would be scared of ghosts as a child.
....

3 My grandparents are always complaining about
teenagers. It gets on my nerves. ....

4 Did you used to get pocket money when you
were very small? ....

5 I used to read a book when my friend called
yesterday. ....

6 You always use to break things. Why are you so
careless? ....

7 People didn't used to travel abroad as much as
they do now. ....

8 Were you sucking your thumb when you were a
baby? ....

9 Where did you use to play when you were a
child? ....

10 I go to school every day and then I use to meet
my friends when I get home. ....

4 Transformations

**Complete the second sentence so that it has
a similar meaning to the first, using the word
given. Do not change the word given. Use
between two and five words.**

1 Maria has a habit of telling lies. **always**
Maria is .... lies.

2 We always went to the beach when we were
young. **used**
We .... to the beach
when we were young.

3 Tom has a habit of breaking things. **is**
Tom .... things.

4 When we were young, we had a habit of playing
with our neighbours' children. **would**
When we were young, we ....
.... with our neighbours' children.

5 I'm not in the habit of going out during the week.
stay
I .... home during
the week.

6 My grandfather had a habit of smoking a pipe in the evenings.
to
My grandfather .... a pipe in the
evenings.

7 As children, we regularly played in the street. **play**
As children, we .... in the street.

8 Peter is never disobedient. **always**
Peter .... what people tell him to do.

Vocabulary ▶ CB p.95

1 Complete the table. Be careful of spelling changes.

Adjective	Comparative	Superlative
happy	1	2 ....
comfortable	3	4 ....
fast	5	6 ....
hard	7	8 ....
good	9	10 ....
bad	11	12 ....
dangerous	13	14 ....
far	15	16 ....
fat	17	18 ....
careful	19	20 ....

Word formation

Fill in the gaps with the correct form of the word in CAPITALS.

1 The .... people get, the less they welcome change. OLD
2 The pace of life is .... these days than in the past. FAST
3 People are a great deal .... nowadays. HEALTH
4 Our roads are much more .... than they were 100 years ago. DANGER
5 One of the .... things about life these days is that people live longer. GOOD
6 People travel much .... than they used to. FAR
7 Pollution is definitely .... now than in the past. BAD
8 People have .... time to relax now. LITTLE
9 Life is certainly .... for young people than it ever was before. GOOD
10 I wonder if people are generally .... than their grandparents used to be. HAPPY

Comparatives and superlatives

Fill in the gaps with the correct form of a word from the list and any other words necessary.

close / quiet / hard / slow / easy / high / sociable / stressful

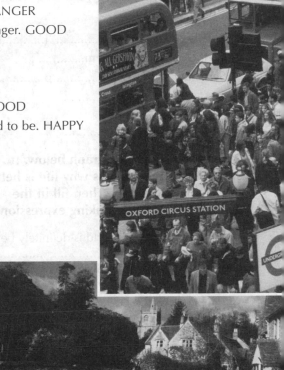

1 It's .... to drive in the country than in the city.
2 Country people have more time to chat so they are often ....
   than people in cities.
3 Life in a village is peaceful; it isn't nearly .... life in the city.
4 There is no noise in our village – it's .... place in the world!
5 Unfortunately, it's a lot .... to find a job in the country
   than in the city.
6 The buildings in New York are some of .... in the world.
7 The pace of life is .... in the country than in a city.
8 The .... I live to the city, the happier I feel.

4 Error correction

Look carefully at each line. Three lines are correct. Tick them. The other lines contain one word which should not be there. <u>Underline</u> it.

> **A BETTER LIFE?**
>
> **0** Don't you hate it when your grandparents insist that life was <u>more</u>
> **00** better in the past? I'm 16 and I think the 21st century is a great time ✔
> **1** to be alive. In fact I think it's the most best, especially if you live in
> **2** a city! Of course, cities are a lot noisier now. And they're definitely
> **3** the more polluted. But they're a great deal more exciting too! Another
> **4** reason I think life is better is because it's much easier than to travel.
> **5** Fifty years ago, travelling by air wasn't nearly as cheap as that it is now.
> **6** These days, teenagers have a lot of more freedom, too. My grandmother
> **7** was never allowed to stay out late or go on holiday alone. My parents
> **8** are much the less strict with me. And what about computers? They didn't
> **9** really exist in my grandparents' day. But I can't imagine life without
> **10** one. The more computer games you have, the better is, in my opinion!

Writing: composition

▶ CB pp.97–98

1 Linking expressions

1 Complete the phrases, starting with the letters given.

1 Finally *or* Last but n................ l................
2 Furthermore *or* What's m................
3 Secondly = In the s................ p................
4 To start with = First o................ a................
5 To sum up *or* In c................

2 Read the short paragraph below. It summarises the reasons why life is better now than in the past. Then fill in the gaps with a suitable linking expression.

Life in the developed world is definitely better now than in the past. (1) ...., people are healthier and live much longer. (2) ...., people don't have to work such long hours in factories and mills any more. (3) ...., they can use machines to do most of the heavy physical work. And, (4) ...., many people earn more money so many can afford holidays and even go abroad to exotic places. (5) ...., life is better in many ways for those of us fortunate enough to live in the wealthier parts of the world.

2 Correct a sample answer

Read the writing task on p.97 of your Coursebook. Look at this sample composition. The student has:

1 forgotten to organise his ideas into paragraphs.
2 not used linking expressions.

Divide the composition into five paragraphs and write it out again in your notebook, adding linking expressions where appropriate.

I think it's very important to keep customs and traditions. Let me tell you why. If we don't keep our different customs, all our countries will become the same. There'll be nothing to see when we go on holiday. Most people enjoy celebrating local customs. Carnivals and festivals are good fun. People can dress up and enjoy themselves. Without them, people won't get together so much. They'll feel isolated and not like a community. I think customs remind us of our history. Without them, we'll forget what makes us a people or a country. People won't know who they are any more and won't be proud of where they come from. I think local customs and traditions play an important part in the life of a country. We should definitely keep them.

3 Writing task

You have been doing a class project on life in the past. Your teacher has asked you to write a composition giving your opinions on the following statement:

Life in the 21st century is better than in the past.

Write your composition in 120–180 words.

Remember to:

• plan your work before you start to write.
• organise your ideas into paragraphs.
• use linking expressions to sequence your ideas.

12 Inventions

Speaking ▶ CB p.99

Functions

> ▶▶ *speaking strategy*
>
> When you are having a discussion with somebody, use phrases like *let's see* and *umm, well* ... to let the other person know that you need time to think. ◀◀

Read the conversation below in which two students are discussing which inventions are the most important. Then put the phrases in *italics* under the correct heading.

1 Asking for an opinion

....

....

2 Disagreeing

....

3 Giving yourself time to think

....

4 Making a suggestion

....

5 Interrupting

....

A: So, *which do you think are the most important?*

B: *Let's start with* the wheel. Without the wheel, we wouldn't have cars or any other form of transport.

A: Yes I agree. And the Internet. The Internet has changed the world, really.

B: Yes, you're right. *What else is important, do you think?'*

A: *Umm, well,* what about the cinema? I mean, we'd really miss that if we didn't have it.

B: *Well yes, but it's not so important really.* We could manage without it. What about the invention of paper? Without it, we wouldn't have books.

A: Yes, that's true.

B: OK, let's see if we agree about our answer ...

A: *Hold on a minute!* We haven't mentioned the telephone. I think it's really important, especially for business.

B: Oh yes, I agree! Now, ...

Reading ▶ CB pp.100–101

1 Sentence completion

Tick the correct option, a) or b). Check your answers by looking at the text on Coursebook p.101.

1 Originally, Bayliss invented his wind-up radio ...
   a) for people in Africa.
   b) for people in Britain.

2 Before the wind-up radio went on sale, most Africans ...
   a) didn't have radios.
   b) couldn't use their radios.

3 The portable car which Vaios has built ...
   a) contains bicycle parts.
   b) has no steering wheel.

4 Vaios's tutors ...
   a) are pleased.
   b) are horrified.

5 Deaf people in US theatres are helped ...
   a) by watching the actors on screen instead of on stage.
   b) by looking at a screen while they are watching the actors on stage.

6 The Q-drum ...
   a) makes it easier to transport water.
   b) makes it easier to purify water.

2 Definitions

Replace the words in *italics* with an appropriate word or phrase from the list.

inventor / employs / come up with / manufacturer / set up / brainwave / designs / electricity is scarce

1 Trevor Bayliss is a British *person who makes, designs or produces new things*. ....

2 Machines are a problem in parts of Africa because *there isn't much electricity*. ....

3 Bayliss had a *sudden very good idea*. ....

4 He couldn't interest any British *company that makes large quantities of goods, using machines* in his invention. ....

5 His company, Baygen, *gives paid work to* disabled people in South Africa. ....

6 When Vaios showed his tutors his *drawings or plans of what his invention would look like*, they didn't think they would work. ....

7 An American called Mr DePew has *thought of* a way to help deaf people. ....

8 The makers of the Q-drum have *started* a factory in Zimbabwe. ....

Grammar ▶ CB p.102, grammar file 16

1 Rewriting

Put the words into the correct order to make sentences.

1 A aeroplane built going is new next of supersonic to be type year

A ....

2 invented bicycle the was When?

....

3 already been computers have invented Pocket-sized

....

4 to is launched going tomorrow satellite new be A

....

5 a be cancer cure for found soon Will?

....

6 be done mobile More on phones research should

....

7 In be built cities sea the may under future the

....

8 safety New be for inventions must tested

....

9 not cloning most countries allowed is Human in

....

10 shut factory the manufacturers made The to were

....

2 Questions in the passive

Use the prompts to make questions.

1 **Question:** Who / television / invent / by?

....

Answer: Logi Baird.

2 **Question:** Where / the first car / manufacture?

....

Answer: In the USA.

3 **Question:** How many mobile phones / sell / recently?

....

Answer: Millions!

4 **Question:** When / cure / find / for Aids?

....

Answer: Very soon, I hope.

5 **Question:** When / the first real computers / build?

....

Answer: During the Second World War.

6 **Question:** Who / telephone / invent by?

....

Answer: By Alexander Graham Bell.

7 **Question:** The new road / still / build?

....

Answer: Yes, they haven't finished it yet.

8 **Question:** Who / penicillin / discover / by?

....

Answer: By Alexander Fleming.

3 The passive

Fill in the gaps with the correct form of the verb in brackets.

1 The aeroplane .... (invent) in the 19th century.

2 The new science laboratory .... (open) next year.

3 The inventor .... (should/ congratulate) on his work.

4 Until now, the machine .... (not / see) by the public.

5 A new helicopter .... (test) at the moment.

6 Scientists .... (tell) about the project yesterday.

7 Coca Cola .... (first / manufacture) in the USA.

8 Prizes .... (award) to the best inventors at tomorrow's Science Exhibition.

4 Transformations

Complete the second sentence so that it has a similar meaning to the first, using the word given. Do not change the word given. Use between two and five words.

1 The engine needs cleaning once a week.

has

The engine .... once a week.

2 They are going to build a new model of car next year.

be

A new model of car .... next year.

3 The price of the computer includes a number of games.

included

A number of games .... in the price of the computer.

4 The government didn't allow him to manufacture his machine.

allowed

He .... his machine.

5 Shops aren't selling as many music cassettes these days.

sold

Not so many music cassettes .... these days.

6 They made the scientist abandon his work.

made

The scientist .... his work.

7 Visitors to the museum are not allowed to touch the exhibits.

must

The exhibits .... visitors.

8 American scientists have just designed the world's most intelligent robot.

been

The world's most intelligent robot .... American scientists.

Vocabulary ▶ CB p.103

1 Parts of appliances

Label the parts of the appliances.

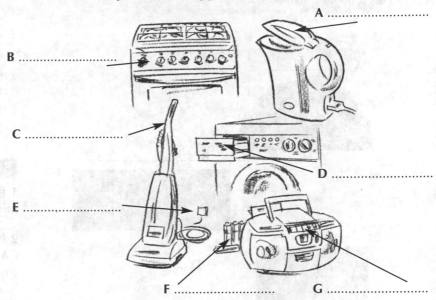

2 Name the object

A

dishwasher   fridge freezer   lawn mower
microwave oven   screwdriver   tin opener
video recorder   mobile phone

B

cook cut fasten keep open record send wash

Fill in the gaps with names of kitchen appliances from Box A and a suitable verb from Box B.

1 You use a .... to .... cans or tins of food.

2 You use a .... to .... programmes from the TV.

3 You use a .... to .... the lawn.

4 You use a .... to .... your food cold or to freeze it.

5 You use a .... to .... something to a wall.

6 You use a .... to .... text messages or to call friends.

7 You use a .... to .... your dirty dishes.

8 You use a .... to .... food quickly.

3 Word sets: shapes

1 Label the shapes, using the words in the box.

> round   triangular   cylindrical   square
> rectangular   semi-circular

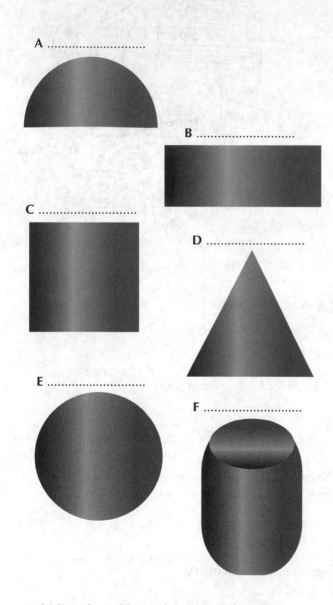

A ....

B ....

C ....

D ....

E ....

F ....

2 Underline the odd word out in each set.

1 plastic, triangular, metal, rubber
2 cylindrical, square, rubber, flat
3 woollen, circular, leather, cotton
4 wooden, gold, rectangular, glass
5 oblong, round, semi-circular, silver

4 Word formation

Follow the instructions below. Write the words in your notebook.

1 Make nouns from these verbs:
   a) *develop*   b) *discover*   c) *communicate*
2 Make adjectives from these nouns:
   a) *invention*   b) *possibility*   c) *profession*
3 Make adjectives from these verbs:
   a) *achieve*   b) *rely*   c) *collapse*   d) *afford*
4 Make nouns from these adjectives:
   a) *able*   b) *intelligent*   c) *technological*

5 Word formation

1 Read the text and <u>underline</u> which type of word is missing from the options given in brackets.

2 Now fill in the missing words. Use the word in CAPITALS underneath to form a word that fits in the gap. Be careful! You may need a negative form! There is an example at the beginning (0).

COMPUTER CAN INVENT PRODUCTS OF ITS OWN

Could robots one day take over the world? That
(0) *possibility.* (*noun* / *adjective*) has come a step
nearer with the **(1)** .... (*noun* / *adjective*)
of 'GP', the first 'creative' computer. For years
(2) .... (*noun* / *adverb*) have been trying
to design **(3)** .... (*adjective* / *adverb*)
computers. These machines would have the
(4) .... (*adjective* / *noun*) to think and act
independently. The latest idea is a computer that can
(5) .... (*adjective* / *adverb*) invent and
design products all by itself. The idea may sound
(6) .... (*adjective* / *adverb*) but it is true.
Professor Koza, the **(7)** .... (*noun* / *adjective*)
of the computer, has tested it against some of the
biggest **(8)** .... (*adjective* / *adverb*)
breakthroughs of the past 100 years. 'It's magical to
watch it invent something in a few days that probably
took someone several years,' he says.

0	POSSIBLE	5	ACTUAL
1	INVENT	6	CREDIBLE
2	SCIENCE	7	DESIGN
3	INTELLIGENCE	8	TECHNOLOGY
4	ABLE		

Writing: report

▶ CB pp.105–106

1 Formal or informal?

Tick the most formal phrase, a) or b).

1   a) We're desperate for videos.
    b) We are rather short of videos.

2   a) Please, please don't get us more books.
    b) I would not recommend getting more books.

3   a) Videos are educational. However, I feel that computer programmes would be even more valuable.
    b) Videos are educational but they're not half as valuable as computer programmes.

4   a) Videos would benefit the greatest number of students.
    b) We'd all rather have videos.

2 Contrast linkers

Fill in the gaps with *although*, *however*, or *in spite of*.

1   .... computer programmes would be enjoyable, I think books would be more useful.

2   .... the fact that we need more books and videos, I think we should use the money to buy computer programmes.

3   We could do with computer programmes. ...., we probably need books and videos more.

4   .... the fact that computer programmes are expensive, I think most people would benefit from them.

5   I think we should buy computer programmes .... they may be the most expensive option.

6   Most people would prefer computer programmes. ...., I would rather we bought books.

3 Correct a sample answer

Read the writing task on p.105 of your Coursebook. Then look at the report that one student wrote and follow the instructions below.

1   Mark where the student should have used contrast linkers.

2   The text has been set out in the wrong format. Write it out again in your notebook in report format, dividing it into sections with headings and making any changes necessary. Remember to start the report correctly. Add contrast linkers where necessary.

Dear directors,

I am writing to tell you which option I think would be best for the school – a new student cafeteria or a new library.

A new library would be very nice. The library we have at the moment is not really adequate. The books are not very old and they aren't in very good condition. There are no computers so we can't find information on the Internet. A new library would cost a lot to build. Computers are very useful. They are expensive.

We really need a new cafeteria. At the moment, we have to eat lunch in the school hall. This means we have to take out tables and put them back every day. A cafeteria would be good for some students. A lot of students go home to eat so they don't need a cafeteria.

The cafeteria would be nice for the reasons I've given. However, I think a new library would benefit the majority of students, which is why I would recommend it.

Yours truly,
....

4 Writing task

Your school has been given a sum of money which is to be spent on either computer programmes or books and videos. You have been asked to write a report for the Principal, describing the benefits of both and saying which you think should be chosen and why.

Write your report in 120–180 words.

Remember to:

• divide your report into sections.
• use expressions to link or contrast your points.

Progress check 3

Grammar

1 Indirect questions

Put the words into the correct order to make indirect questions.

1 English I if know They to wanted was

....

2 closed Could has if me shop tell the you?

....

3 like post office the know to the to way I'd

....

4 Do how is it know much you?

....

5 Could advise to us visit what you?

....

6 Can is me number phone remind what you your?

....

2 Third conditional and wishes

Fill in the gaps using the verb in brackets.

1 I wish I .... (not / miss) the bus this morning. If I .... (leave) home earlier, I .... (catch) it.

2 James wishes he .... (not / argue) with Cilla yesterday. If he .... (not / argue) with her, she .... (not / be) angry with him.

3 Dad wishes .... (not / buy) my brother a motor bike. If he .... (not / buy) it, my brother .... (not / have) the accident.

4 Sarah wishes she .... (save) more money. If she .... (save) enough, her parents .... (might / let) her go to Paris.

5 I wish I .... (read) the TV guide yesterday. I .... (not / miss) the film if I .... (read) it.

6 I wish I .... (not / go) to bed so late last night. If I .... (go) to bed earlier, I .... (not / feel) so sleepy when I got up.

7 My brother wishes he .... (not / miss) football practice. The manager .... (pick) him for the big match if he .... (be) there.

8 I wish you .... (not / tell) me how the film ends. I .... (enjoy) it more if you .... (not / tell) me.

3 Present and past habits

<u>Underline</u> the correct option in each pair. Be careful! Sometimes both verbs are correct.

1 My brother *is always losing / use to lose* things.

2 We *were spending / used to spend* our holidays camping when we were young.

3 Many actors *used to be / would be* shy when they were young.

4 We *were watching / used to watch* TV when the doorbell rang.

5 I *use to go / always go* to bed by 11.00 p.m.

6 I *broke / used to break* my leg on my fifth birthday.

7 John *didn't use to like / wasn't liking* football.

8 When they were small, the children *would go / used to go* swimming in the local river every summer.

4 The passive

Put these sentences into the passive, starting with the words given.

1 Someone is building a new road round the city.
   A new road ....

2 We sell tickets here.
   Tickets ....

3 They gave him a lot of money.
   He ....

4 Someone has invented a motorised scooter.
   A motorised scooter ....

5 They don't let John stay out late.
   John ....

6 They made Paula pay back the money.
   Paula ....

7 The government will introduce a new law.
   A new law ....

8 Elton John opened the new hospital.
   The new hospital ....

Vocabulary

5 Find the mistake

<u>Underline</u> the mistakes in the sentences and write the sentences correctly in your notebook.

1 Spain isn't as big as what China is.

2 Heathrow is the most busy airport in the world.

3 *The Lion King* is the more incredible musical I've seen.

4 The longer I live in this city, the worser I think it is.

5 A youth hostel is a lot more cheaper than a hotel.

6 Life is more noisier than it used to be.

7 My brother is a great deal taller that I am.

8 Boyzone was probably the more popular boy band of the 1990s.

6 Prepositions

Underline the correct word in each pair.

1 I prefer the cinema *to* / *with* the theatre.

2 The director accused us *of* / *in* lying.

3 We insisted *in* / *on* getting our money back.

4 The cameraman finally succeeded *on* / *in* shooting the scene.

5 My parents discouraged me *for* / *from* taking part in dangerous sports.

6 I'll never forgive him *at* / *for* what he did.

7 The bag was full *of* / *with* theatrical costumes.

8 The actress has just come out *of* / *from* her dressing room.

7 Word formation

1 Complete the table.

Verb	Noun	Adjective
encourage	1	2 ....
3	hope	4 ....
5	forgiveness	6 ....
please	7	8 ....
determine	9	10 ....
11	12	disappointed
create	13	14 ....
15	inspiration	16 ....
tolerate	17	18 ....
influence	19	influential

2 Use the words in CAPITALS at the end of each sentence to form a verb, noun or adjective that fits in the gap.

1 The composer, Grieg, was .... by the beauty of his homeland. INSPIRE

2 Martin Luther King fought for greater .... EQUAL

3 Fashion designers have to be extremely .... CREATE

4 The actress was very .... to talk to. PLEASE

5 Missing the film was a big .... DISAPPOINT

6 We're .... to see Robbie Williams, even if we have to queue all night. DETERMINE

7 Mahatma Gandhi begged for greater understanding and .... between all races. TOLERATE

8 Winston Churchill was a highly .... statesman. INFLUENCE

8 Phrasal verbs

Fill in the gaps with the correct verb from the list.

bring / *switch* / *go* / *put* / *split* / *turn*

1 They cancelled the show because the lead singer failed to .... *up.*

2 After ten years together, the band have decided to .... *up* and follow solo careers.

3 At the beginning of a play, the lights .... *out* and the curtain rises.

4 We .... *off* our visit to the theatre because Tom was ill.

5 The pop group, Steps, are going to .... *out* a new record next month.

6 We'd better .... *off* the light and go to sleep now.

9 Choosing the right word

Underline the correct word in each pair.

1 In my school, we learn European languages *like* / *as* French and German.

2 That student looks *like* / *as* a famous actor.

3 Robbie Williams is the one of the most *favourite* / *popular* singers in Britain.

4 Do you like *live* / *life* concerts?

5 Elton John wrote the *music* / *beat* for *The Lion King*.

13 Survival

Speaking ▶ CB p.109

1 Synonyms

Match a verb from Column A with a phrase from Column B.

A	B
1 be adaptable	a) offer to do something
2 cope	b) continue to live (after a dangerous event)
3 miss	c) far away
4 remote	d) feel sad without (something)
5 survive	e) have faith in
6 trust	f) manage
7 volunteer	g) be able to change

2 Word sets: tools

1 Label the objects in the pictures.

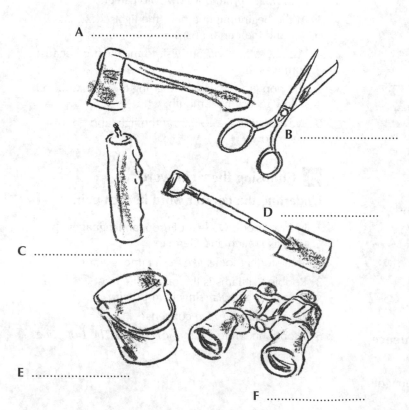

A ....

B ....

C ....

D ....

E ....

F ....

2 Match the sentence halves to make logical sentences.

A	B
1 You use an axe	a) to see distant objects up close.
2 You use a spade	b) to cut paper or string.
3 You use a bucket	c) to dig.
4 You use a pair of scissors	d) to light your way.
5 You use a pair of binoculars	e) to chop wood.
6 You use a candle	f) to store water in.

3 Explanations

▶▶ *speaking strategy*

If you don't know a word in English, don't give up and stop speaking. Try to explain what you mean using other words.

◀◀

Fill in the gaps with words from the list.

word / means / say / mean / don't understand

1 **A:** Would you go to pieces on a desert island?

B: I'm sorry, I .... the question.

2 **A:** Would you make a good castaway?

B: I'm sorry. I don't understand what 'castaway' ....

3 **A:** What qualities do you think you need to survive on a desert island?

B: I think you need to be – how do you .... that – not afraid.

A: Brave

B: Yes, brave, that's the word.

4 **A:** What would you hate most about being on a desert island?

B: I'd hate the er, er, I'm afraid I don't know the .... in English – to be alone.

A: The loneliness?

B: Yes, that's right. I would hate the loneliness.

5 **A:** Would you cope OK on the island?

B: Yes and no. What I .... is, I think I could take care of myself, but I wouldn't be happy. Definitely not.

Reading ► CB pp.110–111

Choosing the right word

Underline the correct word in each pair.

1 The judge decided not to *send / commit* the boys to prison.
2 Instead, they will spend a year in *ordeal / exile* off the Alaskan coast.
3 The robbery was the boys' first *case / offence*.
4 Both boys *pleaded / faced* guilty.
5 It will be at least a year before the boys are *sent / set* free.
6 Everyone hopes that the boys will never *commit / make* another crime.

Words that go together

Fill in the gaps with an appropriate word from the list.

average / basic / common / outside / sleeping / tough

1 The elders decided on quite a .... *punishment* for the young men.
2 The two teenagers will have no contact with the .... *world*.
3 They will be given some very .... *equipment*, but no luxuries.
4 Whales are a .... *sight* in this part of the world.
5 The .... *temperature* here is minus 6 degrees Centigrade.
6 The boys will live in a shelter and will each have a .... *bag*.

3 Prepositions

Fill in the gaps with a preposition from the list.

about / by / in / off / on / with

1 The boys will have to spend 18 months .... the wild.
2 Adrian was banished to an island .... the Alaskan coast.
3 The mountains are covered .... forests.
4 The forests are inhabited .... black bears.
5 Both of the boys will have to live .... their own.
6 They will have to forget .... TV and video games.

Grammar ► CB p.112, grammar file 13

1 Reported statements

Underline the correct option in each pair.

1 The survivor explained that she *has lost / had lost* her way.
2 The girl said she *had spent / spent* three days alone in the forest.
3 She promised she *will / would* never wander off alone again.
4 She admitted that she *had been / has been* been very scared.
5 She told us she *have been / had been* sleeping in the open air.
6 She said she *couldn't / can't* call for help because her mobile phone was broken.

2 Reported questions

Jim has had a caving accident. Report the questions a journalist asked him.

1 How do you feel?
The reporter asked Jim ...*how he felt*............................... .
2 Have you broken any bones?
She asked him ....
3 Can you walk?
The reporter wanted to know if Jim ....
4 How long is it since you ate, Jim?
She asked him how long ....
....
5 Will you have to give up caving in the future, Jim?
She wondered if ....
....
6 Are you going to hospital?
She asked Jim ....
7 When did you realise you were in trouble?
She asked him ....
8 What advice would you give to other cavers, Jim?
She wanted to know ....
....

3 Find the mistake

Two sentences are correct. Tick them. <u>Underline</u> the mistakes in the other sentences and correct them.

1 The reporter asked the climber how long had he been without food.
....

2 His friends said him that they had been very worried.
....

3 The man wanted to know if were the other members of the group safe. ....

4 He explained that he had fallen into a crevasse. ....

5 He wondered whether had he broken his leg. ....

6 The rescuers told him that all his friends had survived.
....

7 He explained that he has dug a hole in the snow to keep warm.
....

8 The climber told that he was beginning to give up hope of rescue.
....

9 Rescuers asked the man how had he managed to find food.
....

10 The climber promised his wife that he will fly home as soon as possible. ....

4 Open cloze

Read the text and think of the word that best fits each space. Use only one word in each space. There is an example at the beginning (0).

SURVIVAL

Dear Linda,

Guess what? We are going to be on TV! The producer rang last night. He said they (0) ....*were*...... making a survival programme and asked if we (1) .... be interested in taking part. He explained that we (2) .... to live alone on a small island for three months. He asked if (3) .... had ever done anything like that before. We (4) .... him we hadn't but that we would (5) .... happy to try it. He told (6) .... that we would be given some basic equipment and a little food and water. He (7) .... us whether we (8) .... all swim. He explained that the sea (9) .... very dangerous in that area. We asked (10) .... to tell us where the camera crew would live. He said they would stay on the mainland and come over to the island every day. He asked us how we (11) .... about being on TV and whether we would be nervous. We assured him that we would be fine. We asked how (12) .... we would earn from the film and he said it would be a lot of money. Isn't it exciting? I can't wait to go!

5 Transformations

Complete the second sentence so that it has a similar meaning to the first sentence, using the word given. Do not change the word given. Use between two and five words.

1 'I've lost my phone!' Sarah said.   **had**
Sarah said .... phone.

2 'Is there anyone you need to telephone?' the journalist asked Alison.   **was**
The journalist asked Alison if .... to telephone.

3 'I've heard your story, Peter,' she said.   **his**
She told .... story.

4 'Did you feel ever feel frightened?' I asked Felix.   **he**
I asked Felix if .... frightened.

5 'I'll fly you to the mainland, Sarah,' the man promised.   **would**
The man promised Sarah that .... to the mainland.

6 'Would you like some water?' the rescuer asked.   **wanted**
The rescuer asked us .... water.

7 'I've had a great time,' Sam told us.   **had**
Sam told .... a great time.

8 'I'm happy I'm home,' he said.   **be**
He said that .... home.

Vocabulary ▶ CB p.113

1 Choosing the right word

Complete the sentences below with the correct word. Use each word once only.

> dig   chop

1 I'll .... some wood and make up a fire.

2 I need to .... a hole for the tree.

> hunt   chase

3 If we want food, we'll have to .... animals.

4 Cats always .... mice.

> lose   miss

5 We must be careful not to .... our way in the forest.

6 Don't .... the turning – it's on the left.

2 Phrasal verbs

Match the sentence halves to make logical sentences.

A	B
1 Can anyone come up	a) across some sign of habitation.
2 I hope we come	b) over what has happened.
3 We'll just have to carry	c) of coffee.
4 We'll have to make do	d) with a solution?
5 We'll need time to get	e) on walking.
6 We've completely run out	f) with water.

3 Word formation

What part of speech are the words below?

1 safe = *adjective*

2 safety = ...

3 rely = ...

4 survive = ...

5 advise = ...

6 advice = ...

7 difficult = ...

8 difficulty = ...

9 unfortunately = ...

10 disappearance = ...

11 suitable = ...

12 appear = ...

13 reliable = ...

14 survival = ...

15 rescuer = ...

4 Word formation

Use the word in CAPITALS underneath to form a word that fits in the space. There is an example at the beginning (0).

COUPLE SURVIVE LIFT ORDEAL

An elderly couple are now (0) .....*safe*............. in hospital after spending a fortnight trapped in a lift. The couple, who are both in their 70s, were having (1) .... climbing the stairs. They asked their doctor for (2) .... and he suggested getting a lift. So the couple looked for the most (3) .... design they could find and had it installed.

(4) ...., the lift they chose was not very (5) .... One day, when they were both inside, the lift doors stuck. They shouted and banged on the door but there was nobody to hear them. Two weeks passed before a neighbour noticed their (6) ....

When police broke into their house, they found the couple weak but alive. The couple told their (7) .... that they hadn't eaten or drunk anything for days. The police said their (8) .... was a miracle.

0	SAVE	**5**	RELY
1	DIFFICULT	**6**	APPEAR
2	ADVISE	**7**	RESCUE
3	SUIT	**8**	SURVIVE
4	FORTUNATE		

Writing: story ▶ CB pp.115–116

1 Adding interest

<u>Underline</u> the most vivid word in each pair.

1 We had a *very nice / fantastic* holiday in the Spanish Pyrenees last year.
2 The views from our hotel were *spectacular / good*.
3 The staff were *marvellous / very nice* and made us feel very welcome.
4 But something *dreadful / bad* happened on our second day.
5 We were skiing in the mountains when there was a *bad / terrible* avalanche.
6 When we heard the first noises, we all stopped and *looked / stared*.
7 Then everyone *rushed / went* to escape from the falling snow.
8 We were all *terrified / afraid*.
9 'Oh no,' my sister *said / screamed*. 'It's coming this way.'
10 I *grabbed / took* her hand and skied as fast as I could.

2 Correct a sample answer

Read the exam task on p.115 of your Coursebook. Then look at the story that one student wrote and follow the instructions below.

1 The student has made six tense mistakes. Find them and <u>underline</u> them.
2 The student has used the word *nice* six times! Rewrite the story in your notebook, replacing *nice* with a different word and correcting the tense mistakes.

A few months ago my friend James and I went for a walk. We live in a <u>nice</u> valley. There is a <u>nice</u> path up the mountains and we've gone up there.

We were walking a long way. It was a <u>nice</u> day but there were no other people on the mountain. Eventually, we sat down to have a <u>nice</u> drink. I put my hat on the ground but the wind blew it away. It stopped at the edge of the rocks. James went to get it when suddenly his foot slipped. He was starting to fall!

I ran over. 'James,' I called, 'are you all right?' He was stuck on a ledge, halfway down the mountain. His ankle was broken and he couldn't move. What can I do? There was nobody to help, and it was getting dark. I couldn't leave James alone.

I've stayed with James for hours. It wasn't a <u>nice</u> experience. Meanwhile our parents had called the police and they've sent a rescue helicopter to look for us. When we saw it, we felt really <u>nice</u>. The nightmare was over. We were safe at last.

3 Writing task

Your local newspaper is running a writing competition. The lucky winners will receive a sum of money. The story must end with the words:

> Peter sighed with relief. Everything would be all right, after all.

Write your story in 120–180 words.

Remember to:

- brainstorm the plot before you start writing. You can use the picture below to give you ideas. Ask yourself questions like these:
  1 Which sentences must you use to end the story?
  2 Who is Peter? Who else was involved in this story?
  3 Something went wrong and it made Peter feel afraid / nervous / worried. What was it?
  4 When / Where / Why did this happen? What was Peter doing? Describe the background to the story.
  5 How did people react?
  6 What happened in the end to make Peter sigh with relief?
- make your story interesting by using vivid vocabulary to describe details.
- include some direct speech (but not too much!)
- make sure you check your work for grammar, spelling or punctuation mistakes.

14 Animal kingdom

Speaking ▶ CB p.117

Introducing examples

Look at the phrases in the box and write them under the correct heading. Then read the conversation and fill in the gaps.

Besides, …	I've read that …
For instance, …	You can see in the picture that …

A Describing a picture

....

B Giving examples

....

C Adding another reason

....

D Giving reasons for your opinion

....

Question: Is it OK to hunt animals?

A: I think hunting is sometimes OK. In some countries, like Alaska for example, people have to hunt or they would starve.

B: But I think the reasons for hunting are important. I mean, *you* (1) .... those people are hunting just for fun. That's cruel.

A: Yes, but sometimes we need to control the numbers of animals. *For* (2) ...., if there are too many animals and not enough food in one place, it's better to shoot some animals – otherwise all the animals will die of hunger.

B: OK, but that's a special situation. (3) ...., I don't think that's really hunting. People usually hunt for pleasure – and they don't care what happens to wildlife. Think about whales, for instance. *I've* (4) .... some species will soon become extinct unless people stop hunting them.

A: Yes, that's true.

Reading ▶ CB pp.118–119

1 Word sets: diving

1 Label the pictures with words from the list.

snorkel / bubbles / wetsuit / rope / cage / mask

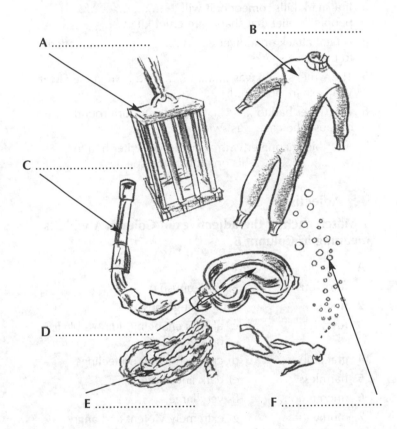

A ....

B ....

C ....

D ....

E ....

F ....

2 Match a phrase from Column A with a word from Column B to make logical sentences.

A	B
1 Divers are safe from sharks if they stay in a	a) snorkel.
2 The cage is tied to the boat with a strong	b) bubbles.
3 To keep warm underwater, divers wear a	c) cage.
4 A diver's face is completely covered by a	d) mask.
5 While underwater, a diver can breathe air through a	e) rope.
6 When a diver is underwater, you can see lots of oxygen	f) wetsuit.

2 **Verbs**

Fill in the gaps with a verb from the list. You may need to change the form of the verb.

reinforce / undermine / provoke / jolt / revise / swallow / struggle

1 Sharks sometimes .... things like shoes and driving licences.

2 Sharks don't usually attack people unless they are ....

3 If a shark kills someone, it will .... people's belief that sharks are cruel killers.

4 A fatal attack on a diver could .... efforts to conserve sharks.

5 The writer's cage was .... when the Great White shark appeared.

6 The writer had to .... to turn round because the cage was swinging.

7 After his encounter with a shark, the writer had to .... his opinion of the species.

3 **Adjectives**

1 Match each of the adjectives in Column A with its meaning in Column B.

A	B
1 ferocious	a) rare, unusual
2 huge	b) not dangerous
3 fussy	c) always changing, impossible to be sure of
4 graceful	d) cruel, showing no feelings
5 harmless	e) dark and dirty
6 uncommon	f) very large
7 murky	g) extremely violent and angry
8 unpredictable	h) careful, choosy
9 cold-blooded	i) threatening
10 aggressive	j) smooth and attractive

2 Underline the correct word in each pair.

1 The water was very *fussy / murky*.

2 Some species of sharks are *harmless / uncommon* but the Great White is a killer.

3 In spite of its size, the Great White is a surprisingly *graceful / ferocious* swimmer.

4 The shark's behaviour is *cold-blooded / unpredictable* so you never know where it will appear next.

5 The Great White looks *huge / aggressive* when you compare it to most other sharks which are much smaller.

Grammar ▶ CB p.120, grammar file 15

1 **Sentence completion**

Tick the correct option, a) or b).

1 My uncle offered …
   a) to buy me a goldfish.
   b) me to buy a goldfish.

2 Sonya admitted …
   a) that she had lost the dog.
   b) to lose the dog.

3 Alexandra suggested …
   a) us to go to the zoo.
   b) that we should go to the zoo.

4 Dad threatened …
   a) giving away our hamster.
   b) to give away our hamster.

5 Tom asked …
   a) that I feed his parrot.
   b) me to feed his parrot.

6 Tanya denied …
   a) to leave the cage open.
   b) leaving the cage open.

7 The teacher asked George …
   a) to not bring his pets to school.
   b) not to bring his pets to school.

8 My little cousin refused …
   a) to show me her pet lamb.
   b) showing me her pet lamb.

2 **Reported statements**

Put the sentences into reported speech, starting with the words given.

1 'Why don't we buy the dog a new collar?'
   My sister suggested ....

2 'OK! I'll look for your hamster.'
   My friend promised ....

3 'I wouldn't put your hand in the cage, if I were you'.
   The attendant advised ....

4 'I'm going to give the dog away unless someone takes it for a walk!'.
   My mother threatened ....

5 'Don't go near the snake!'
   The warden warned us ....

6 'No, we didn't leave the gate open.'
   The children denied ....

3 Make sentences

Match the sentence halves to make logical sentences.

A
1 My brother refused
2 Peter suggested
3 Our neighbours admitted
4 Mum warned me not to
5 Alicia complained
6 My friends advised

B
a) bring a rat into the house.
b) that the cat made her sneeze.
c) to feed my hamster.
d) me to keep away from the bull.
e) going to see the horses.
f) that their dog had stolen the meat.

4 Open cloze

Read the text and think of the word that best fits each space. Use only one word in each space. There is an example at the beginning (0).

AN UNWELCOME VISITOR

When Lucy the tarantula disappeared **(0)** .....*from*.............. the local pet shop, she caused **(1)** .... lot of excitement. The pet shop owner searched everywhere **(2)** .... he couldn't find the spider. Meanwhile Mrs Butler, one of his regular customers, **(3)** .... driving along the high street with her daughter, Lisa. They **(4)** .... bought a hamster from the pet shop earlier that morning, together with a box and straw. They were on their way to McDonald's where Mrs Butler had promised **(5)** .... buy Lisa some lunch. They **(6)** .... parking the car outside the restaurant **(7)** .... Lisa screamed. She said **(8)** .... was a huge spider crawling up the door. Mrs Butler warned her daughter **(9)** .... to touch the spider because it might **(10)** .... poisonous. She ran into McDonald's for help. The manager advised **(11)** .... to phone the local zoo. But by the **(12)** .... help arrived, Lucy had disappeared again! The question was, what should they do next?

Vocabulary ▶ CB p.121

1 Word formation

Fill in the gaps with the correct form of the word in CAPITALS. In this exercise, you will need to form nouns.

1 I get a lot of .... out of watching wild animals. PLEASE
2 The World Wildlife Fund works in the field of animal .... CONSERVE
3 Boa constrictors have incredible .... STRONG
4 Some animals enjoy a very long .... LIVE
5 Zoologists study animal .... BEHAVE
6 You need a lot of .... when you are observing wildlife. PATIENT
7 The .... that many animals may become extinct is terrible. POSSIBLE
8 I was surprised at my brother's .... of pet. CHOOSE

2 Verb + preposition

Fill in the gaps with a preposition from the list. The verbs are in *italics* to help you.

for / from / on / to / against / to / of / for

1 My brother *insists* .... keeping his pet mouse in his bedroom.
2 The vet *warned* me .... buying a tarantula.
3 We couldn't *prevent* the dog .... chasing the sheep.
4 Mum *blamed* the dog .... digging up her flowers.
5 I *object* .... being woken up by my neighbour's dog.
6 We *suspect* that man .... stealing our cat.
7 Keeping a snake as a pet doesn't *appeal* .... me.
8 I've never *forgiven* my sister .... dropping a spider on me.

3 Opposites

Write the opposite of the words in Column A in Column B.

A Word	B Opposite	A Word	B Opposite
1 common	....	6 predictable	....
2 fit	....	7 safe	....
3 legal	....	8 suitable	....
4 loyal	....	9 true	....
5 patient	....	10 understood	....

4 Lexical cloze

Read the text and decide which answer A, B, C or D best fits each space.
There is an example at the beginning (0).

0	A demands	B wants	C insists	D looks

DOG HANDLER

Bruno Holden works for the police. As an experienced dog handler, he
(0) ..C... on complete obedience from the dogs he trains. 'If a policeman
(1) .... someone of **(2)** .... a crime,' Bruno explains, 'he will usually arrest
him. It is easier to make an arrest with a dog present. A good police dog
should **(3)** .... a criminal from escaping but it should **(4)** .... attack without
a signal from its owner.' Bruno's dogs look very gentle. **(5)** ...., he warns me
(6) .... stroking them. 'They are **(7)** .... training,' he says, 'so you can't
(8) .... them if they bark and jump up at people sometimes.'

The dogs stay with Bruno for about six months. They sleep in the kitchen.
'Luckily, my wife doesn't **(9)** .... to them being there,' he says. Before I
leave, he **(10)** .... that I join him in the garden 'for a private show'. I watch
(11) .... the biggest dog pretends to arrest me. I stand there, paralysed with
fear until the dog **(12)** .... me go. At that moment I **(13)** .... myself to obey
the law at all costs. I never want to be that close to a police dog again!

1	A suspects	B believes	C thinks	D realises
2	A making	B carrying	C committing	D achieving
3	A refuse	B prevent	C warn	D make
4	A ever	B hardly	C never	D scarcely
5	A Although	B In spite	C However	D Since
6	A for	B against	C to	D from
7	A still	B yet	C more	D during
8	A accuse	B complain	C blame	D tell
9	A object	B mind	C forbid	D deny
10	A offers	B tells	C asks	D suggests
11	A at	B during	C for	D while
12	A allows	B admits	C lets	D permits
13	A promise	B threaten	C suggest	D agree

Writing: article ▶ CB pp.123–124

1 Reason and result

<u>Underline</u> the correct option in each pair.

1 I would love to own a snake *so / because* I think they're fascinating animals.

2 *As / So* I want to see a tiger, I will probably have to go to India.

3 Dolphins are magical creatures. *That's why / So* I want to see them in the wild.

4 Gorillas are endangered animals *as / so* only a few people get to see them close-up.

5 *As / So* tarantulas are poisonous, they're dangerous to handle.

6 I love penguins *so / as* I'd like to visit Alaska.

2 Topic sentences

Tick the most vivid topic sentence in each pair.

1 a) Who hasn't dreamt of seeing their favourite animal up close in the wild?

   b) Most of us would like to see our favourite animal up close in the wild.

2 a) Imagine how it must feel to swim with dolphins.

   b) It must be nice to swim with dolphins.

3 a) I would like to go right up to a family of gorillas.

   b) Just think how wonderful it must be to go right up to a family of gorillas.

4 a) Wouldn't it be fantastic to watch a tiger creep through the jungle?

   b) I would enjoy seeing a tiger creep through the jungle.

3 Correct a sample answer

Read the writing task on p.123 of your Coursebook.

The student has written a topic sentence at the start of each paragraph but these are not very vivid. Write the article again, making some of the topic sentences more vivid.

> ### The Perfect Pet
>
> Maybe you are thinking of buying a pet. If you are, you should buy a cat. I'll tell you the reason.
>
> Cats are friendly. They sit on your knee in the evening and keep you company. They are soft and furry and you can stroke them. This is good for them and it's good for you too, because it makes you relax.
>
> Cats are easy to look after. You don't have to take them out for a walk or bath them. They don't chase the neighbours either. If you go away for a holiday, you can leave them at home and ask your neighbour to feed them.
>
> Cats don't need much space. You can easily keep a cat in a flat. (Dogs need a big garden so they're much more trouble!) A cat will keep the mice away too.
>
> All in all, a cat makes a perfect pet. Believe me. I've got five cats and they're terrific.

4 Writing task

You see this competition in a wildlife magazine.

> ## COMPETITION
>
> *Which two animals would you most like to watch in the wild? Why?*
>
> **Write an article about the topic above.**
> The writer of the best article will win a wildlife holiday.

Write your article in 120–180 words.

Remember to:

- give examples and details to back up your statements.
- make sure you involve your reader, maybe by asking questions.

15 Fashion

Speaking ▶ CB p.125

1 Expressing opinions

Look at the pictures and complete each caption with a phrase from the box.

> I'd definitely have …
> I wouldn't be seen dead …
> I'm very choosy …
> I don't mind …
> I can't stand …

▶▶ *speaking strategy*
When you give an opinion, try to vary the way you use the language. ◀◀

2 What's the word?

Put the letters in the right order to make an item of clothing. (You can find all of the items on p.125 of your Coursebook.)

1 cfras
   (Clue: It's worn on the head or round the neck.)
   Answer: s.*carf*..........

2 swtaitoca
   (Clue: It's sleeveless and it's part of a suit.)
   Answer: **w**................

3 rtaierns
   (Clue: You wear them on your feet.)
   Answer: **t**...............

4 rtksi
   (Clue: It's worn by a woman.)
   Answer: **s**...............

5 srtuores
   (Clue: these have legs.)
   Answer: **t**...............

1 '.......................................
in a suit.'

2 '...
wearing the same as my sister.'

3 '..
about what I buy.'

4 '...
baggy trousers.'

5 '...
a stud in my nose.'

Reading ▶ CB pp.126–127

1 Verbs

1 Match a verb from Column A with a verb of similar meaning from Column B.

A	B
1 affect	a) calm
2 dye	b) follow
3 dictate	c) frighten
4 pursue	d) influence
5 distinguish	e) represent
6 scare	f) change the colour of
7 soothe	g) show the difference
8 symbolise	h) control

2 Now fill in the gaps with the correct form of verbs from Column A.

1 Long ago, people painted their faces to .... off bad spirits.

2 Cosmetics were first used to .... between men and women.

3 Young people who decorate their bodies are .... their ancestors' ideal of beauty.

4 The power in clothes .... the people around you.

5 The colour green can .... the nerves.

6 The Aztecs .... their textiles many different colours.

7 In ancient Egypt, red .... blood.

8 Nowadays, fashion .... the clothes we wear, not money.

2 Definitions

Replace the words in *italics* with an appropriate word or phrase from the list.

wealthy / rituals / cosmetics / textiles / dazzled / sorrow / ripe / go for

1 There is such a range of colours in fashion departments, you may be *unable to see for a short time*. ....

2 You can buy many different *fabrics* in the shops. ....

3 In the past, people used *make-up* to distinguish between different tribes. ....

4 Yellow is the colour of *mature* corn. ....

5 In Asia, white was the colour of *sadness*. ....

6 Blue and red used to be associated with religious *ceremonies*. ....

7 When you choose clothes, you should *choose* the colours that suit you best. ....

8 These days, you don't need to be *rich* to look fashionable. ....

3 Choosing the right word

Complete the sentences below with the correct word. Use each word once only.

> paint   decorate   dye

1 You can .... fabrics to change their colours.

2 People used to .... their faces and bodies.

3 Some girls use removable transfers to .... their arms and legs.

> clash   suit

4 Some colours ...., which means they don't go together.

5 You should wear colours that .... you.

4 Prepositions

Fill in the gaps with the correct preposition from the list. Some words are in *italics* to help you.

between / in / into / under / with / within

1 You can buy clothes in every colour .... *the sun*.

2 Body painting is coming back .... *fashion*.

3 People painted their faces to *distinguish* .... men and women.

4 .... *ancient times*, people painted their bodies to scare away evil spirits.

5 You should wear colours that *go* .... your hair colour.

6 Nowadays, style is .... *reach* of us all.

Grammar ▶ CB p.128, grammar files 16,17

Impersonal statements

Match the sentence halves to make logical sentences.

A

1 The ancient Celts are known
2 Blue jeans are said
3 Versace is believed
4 Cleopatra is considered
5 The colour green is claimed
6 In traditional societies, body painting was believed

B

a) to be soothing.
b) to scare off evil spirits.
c) to be going out of fashion.
d) to have been a very beautiful woman.
e) to have been one of the world's most successful designers.
f) to have painted their bodies.

Choosing the right word

Underline the correct option in each pair.

1 I have just been to the hairdresser's *to cut my hair / to have my hair cut*.
2 Elton John is said *having / to have* millions of clothes.
3 The Inca rulers are known *to have worn / to wear* clothes made of gold.
4 I went to the dentist *to have filled a tooth / to have a tooth filled*.
5 Cleopatra is thought *to be / to have been* less beautiful than historians claimed.
6 Are you going to *have dyed your hair / have your hair dyed*?
7 It *is known / knows* that primitive people wore animal skins.
8 My friend is going to have *his arm tattooed / tattooed his arm*.

3 *have / get* + object + past participle

Rewrite these sentences, using *have* or *get*.

1 A tailor is making my father a dinner jacket.
My father is getting ....*a dinner jacket made*....... .

2 Someone has stolen my sister's bracelet.
My sister has ......*had her bracelet stolen*............ .

3 I got someone to alter my trousers.
I got ....

4 A florist is going to deliver the flowers to us.
We ....

5 A reporter took Jane's photo.
Jane ....

6 The hairdresser is dyeing my hair.
I'm ....

7 They have dry-cleaned my jacket.
I ....

8 They are tattooing Paul's arm.
Paul ....

4 Transformations

Complete the second sentence so that it has a similar meaning to the first sentence, using the word given. Do not change the word given. Use between two and five words.

1 Everyone thinks that Donna will become a model.
expected
Donna .... a model.

2 The hairdresser cut my hair yesterday.
had
I .... yesterday.

3 They think that tongue studs can cause infections.
believed
It .... tongue studs can cause infections.

4 People consider that tattoos are fashionable.
be
Tattoos .... fashionable.

5 The tailor is going to shorten my trousers.
have
I'm going to the tailor's to ....
....

6 They know that Romans wore togas.
have
Romans are known ....
.... togas.

7 People say that thieves have stolen jewellery worth thousands of pounds.
said
Thieves ....
jewellery worth thousands of pounds.

8 The beautician pierced my ears last week.
had
I .... last week.

9 A fashion expert designed my sister's dress.
had
My sister .... by a fashion expert.

10 People say that Kate Moss is one of the world's best models.
thought
Kate Moss ....
one of the world's best models.

Vocabulary ▶ CB p.129

1 Word sets: clothes

Look at the words in the list. Write M next to items usually worn by men, W next to those usually worn by women and B next to those often worn by both.

blouse	*tights*	*earrings* ....
overalls	*trainers*	*cardigan* ....
waistcoat	*dinner jacket*	*scarf* ....
cap	*dress*	*brooch* ....

2 Adjective order

▶▶ *How many adjectives?*

Don't use more than two or three adjectives together when you describe something.

1 The pop star was wearing a really sensational, bright green, Chinese silk outfit. ✗

2 The pop star was wearing a really sensational outfit. It was bright green and made of Chinese silk. ✔

◀◀

1 Look at the words in the box. Put them under the correct heading. Write the table in your notebook.

silk   pretty   navy   checked   tight   Russian   loose   amazing   cotton   purple   awful   maroon   Brazilian   leather   denim   linen   high-heeled

1 opinion ➔	**2 size / shape** ➔	**3 colour**
fantastic	small	dark green

4 pattern ➔	**5 origin** ➔	**6 material**
striped	French	satin

2 Two sentences are correct. Tick them. Write the other sentences correctly in your notebook, putting the adjectives in the correct order.

1 Jane was dressed in a cotton, long-sleeved green shirt.

2 The singer was wearing a short, black cotton jacket.

3 The model wore fantastic, leather red trousers.

4 I'm wearing a pale grey woollen sweater and blue denim jeans.

5 Olivia was dressed in a blue, silk long dress.

6 My boyfriend wore linen, baggy long trousers.

3 Choosing the right word

Complete the sentences below with the correct word. Use each word once only.

carry   get dressed   wear

1 Do you usually .... jeans in your free time?

2 I don't want to .... an umbrella all day.

3 I always .... before I have breakfast.

match   suit   fit

4 Does this colour .... me, do you think?

5 I've got fat so my clothes don't .... me.

6 That jacket doesn't .... your trousers.

go with   put on   clash

7 Shall I .... this blue jacket?

8 Those colours .... You shouldn't wear them together.

9 That scarf doesn't .... your jacket.

4 Open cloze

Read the text and think of the word that best fits each space. Use only one word in each space. There is an example at the beginning (0).

FASHION MODEL SOPHIE DAHL

As a child, Sophie Dahl always imagined she would end (0) .....*up*......... writing like her grandfather, Roald Dahl. Then (1) .... was spotted by *Vogue* magazine, crying (2) .... a London street. Within weeks she (3) .... signed a contract with a top model agency. Sophie was very tall (4) .... plump. At (5) ...., stylists complained that (6) .... couldn't find any clothes to (7) .... her. For her first job, embarrassingly, she had to get (8) .... in outfits held together with pins! But shoppers were delighted. Sophie modelled outfits that all women could (9) ...., whether they were fat or thin. 'Sophie always (10) .... good in everything she (11) .... on,' a top fashion reporter says. 'She has revolutionised the industry and brought curves back (12) .... fashion.'

Writing: composition

▶ CB pp.131–132

1 Balanced writing

<u>Underline</u> the correct option in each pair.

1 There are good reasons why people are so keen on fashion. *At first / In the first place*, people notice you more if you dress well.

2 I think fashion is important. *However / On the one hand*, some people spend too much money on it.

3 I think you can waste a lot of time on fashion. *What's more / On the other hand*, it's important to look good.

4 *In conclusion / At last*, I would say that it is important not to spend all your time and money on clothes.

2 Correct a sample answer

Read the writing task on p.131 of your Coursebook. Then look at the composition that one student wrote and follow the instructions below.

1 The student has not separated his arguments into separate paragraphs.

2 His introduction and conclusion are very poor.

Write the letter out again in your notebook, separating the arguments for and against into different paragraphs, and improving the introduction and conclusion. Use linking expressions where appropriate.

> I agree with part of this statement.
> I think young people should be able to wear the clothes they want, most of the time. Young people want to look like other people in their group. They don't want to look different. If their parents choose their clothes, their friends will laugh at them. The only problem is, some young people want to spend too much on clothes. They want designer labels. Other kids want things like studs and tattoos, which might not be a good idea. They might be sorry when they get older. So sometimes parents know better. On the other hand, most kids are sensible. If they are allowed to choose, they won't buy stupid things. However, if they have to wear what their parents say and they look old-fashioned, they will lose confidence and this could affect their lives in a bad way.
> To sum up, I agree with the question, but only in part.

3 Writing task

Your class has been discussing the latest fashions in clothes. Your teacher has asked you to write a composition outlining the arguments for and against this statement:

> Young people worry too much about fashion and clothes.

Write a composition of 120–180 words.

Remember to:

- brainstorm the plot before you start writing. Ask yourself questions like these:

1 Do you worry what you wear and what the latest fashions are?

2 Why do young people often want fashionable clothes? How important is it to 'keep up with the gang'?

3 Do you think young people generally have more money than people did in the past? Is it a good idea to spend a lot on clothes and fashion? Why / Why not?

4 Are designer labels expensive? What happens to young people who can't afford them?

5 Do you think young people are influenced by advertisements for clothes? Should advertisers stop targeting young people so much? Why / Why not?

6 Do you think some young people worry too much about clothes and fashion? Why / Why not? Is it possible to be happy without buying lots of new clothes?

- divide your arguments for and against into separate paragraphs.

- use linking expressions where appropriate.

16 Our environment

Speaking ▶ CB p.133

Discussing options

Fill in the gaps with words or phrases from the list.

because / better / decided / do you think /
important / should definitely /
need to think / we must

A: So, we have to decide the three best ways to save energy. Let's see, what (1) ....? What about using public transport instead of going by car? It's much better for the environment.

B: I'm sure you're right because cars cause a lot of pollution. Yes, (2) .... put that in the leaflet.

A: And what do you think about keeping your heating turned down? I think this is very (3) .... because heating uses up a lot of energy.

B: I'm not so sure about that. It depends on other people in the house. Old people could get very cold. I think maybe switching off lights is a (4) .... idea.

A: Yes, I'm sure you're right (5) .... we all forget to do that.

B: OK, so we've (6) .... : using public transport and switching off lights, yes? So, we (7) .... of one more thing.

A: What do you think about recycling?

B: Yes, it's a great idea! We (8) .... include that.

Reading ▶ CB pp.134–135

1 Words that go together

1 Match a word from Column A with a word from Column B.

A	B
1 public	a) city
2 a bike/bus	b) plate
3 a number	c) jam
4 a parking	d) space
5 the inner	e) lane
6 a traffic	f) transport

2 Fill in the gaps with an appropriate word.

1 My teacher was late because he got stuck in a ....
2 We drove round for hours before we could find a .... to leave the car in.
3 Cyclists can avoid the traffic if they use the special ....
4 The level of pollution is much higher in the ....
5 It's better for the environment if you use .... rather than cars.
6 It's illegal to drive your car without a .... to identify it.

2 Definitions

Replace the words in *italics* with an appropriate word or phrase from the list.

pick them up / switch / banned / coped / heads for / lift /
fare / outskirts

1 This article looks at how five cities have *dealt successfully* with traffic problems. ....
2 It's easy to *change* from one bus route to another in Curitiba. ....
3 In Curitiba, there is a fixed *price for a ticket* on all the buses. ....
4 In Milan, everyone *goes towards* the city on foot. ....
5 In Athens, when pollution is high, all cars are *forbidden* from entering the city centre. ....
6 In future, it may be possible to *remove* traffic restrictions in Athens. ....
7 In Lüneburg, there is a park and ride on the *edge* of the town. ....
8 In Lüneburg, people can leave their bags in a central place and *collect them* when they leave. ....

3 Word sets: types of people

Complete the definitions with words from the list.

authorities / commuters / employees / pedestrians / residents / the disabled / employers

1 .... (n.) people who live in an area

2 .... (n.) people who cannot use part of their body

3 .... (n.) people who work for someone

4 .... (n.) people who employ others to work for them

5 .... (n.) people who are on foot

6 .... (n.) people who are in charge, such as government officials

7 .... (n.) people who travel to work regularly

4 Prepositions

Fill in the gaps with a correct preposition from the list.

at / on / by / on / outside / by / on / under

1 Nearly 75 per cent of commuters in Curitiba travel .... bus.

2 Nearly everyone in Milan parks .... the city centre and then walks in.

3 They park .... the edge of the restricted area.

4 In Holland, the number of car owners rose by 15 per cent .... average.

5 The majority of people travel .... bike.

6 In Athens, people can only use their cars .... certain days.

7 Fifty per cent of cars must stay .... home each day.

8 A new railway system is .... construction.

Grammar ▶ CB p.136, grammar file 8

1 Future perfect

Make logical sentences by matching words and phrases from each of the columns A, B and C. Then write them underneath.

A	B	C
By the year 2060,	1 computers	may have found a cure for cancer.
	2 doctors	may have built robots that can feel emotion.
	3 self-cleaning cars	will have become extinct.
	4 more animals	will have risen by a few centimetres.
	5 sea levels	will have become smaller and more powerful.
	6 people on Earth	may have been discovered.
	7 new planets	will probably have been invented.
	8 engineers	may have made contact with life on other planets.

1 ....

2 ....

3 ....

4 ....

5 ....

6 ....

7 ....

8 ....

2 Choosing the right word

<u>Underline</u> the correct option in each pair.

1 By the year 2050, people *may be living / may live* on the moon.

2 By the time most of us are 80, the world *will change / will have changed* completely.

3 By the year 2050, we *may have discovered / may discover* new galaxies.

4 I hope that in 20 years from now we *will be stopping / will have stopped* polluting the Earth.

5 This time next year, I *will study / will be studying* environmental science at university.

6 Will you still *be learning / learn* English in two years time?

7 By the start of the next century, our climate *will have changed / will change* completely.

8 This time next week, we *will listen / will be listening* to someone from the World Wildlife Fund.

3 Which future?

Fill in the gaps with the correct form of the verb in brackets.

1 **A:** .... (you/be) in class tomorrow?

   B: No. While you're having your lesson, I .... (have) a job interview!

2 **A:** Do you think you .... (get married) by this time next year?

   B: No way! I'm never getting married!

3 **A:** John's giving a party tonight.

   B: Yes. I .... (see) you there!

4 **A:** Do you think scientists .... (discover) other life forms in our universe?

   B: I don't know. They might!

5 **A:** Do you think you .... (still/come) to this class in two years' time?

   B: Yes, I probably will.

6 **A:** By this time next year .... (you/learn) a lot more English?

   B: I certainly hope so!

4 Future simple or future continuous?

Underline the correct option in each pair.

1 The pilot says *we'll be landing/we'll land* in ten minutes.

2 This time next year *I'll lie/be lying* on a tropical beach.

3 Don't worry! I'm sure *you'll pass/you'll be passing* your driving test.

4 I can't ring you at 11 a.m. tomorrow because *I'll sit/I'll be sitting* in the dentist's chair then!

5 Take care or *you'll drop/you'll be dropping* that glass!

6 I'll *be learning/learn* English this time next week.

7 When you come out of your class, *I'll wait/I'll be waiting* for you in the Hall.

8 As soon as I hear any news, *I'll tell/I'll be telling* you.

5 Error correction

Look carefully at each line. Four lines are correct. Tick them. The other lines each have a word which should not be there. Underline it. There are two examples at the beginning (0) and (00).

WHAT THE FUTURE HOLDS

0	How do you imagine the future? In just twenty years from now, experts ✔
00	tell us, life will be <u>probably</u> very different. By 2020, scientists will
1	have been invented a tiny ear-piece that can translate foreign languages
2	instantly. In the thirty years' time, we may be taking our holidays in
3	luxury 'space' hotels which will be go round the Earth. By the year
4	2030, we'll all will be living longer. By then, doctors will probably
5	have learnt how to cure illnesses such as cancer and AIDS. Scientists may
6	they also have learnt how to use genetics to treat disease. A human being
7	may even have to been cloned. By 2030, most people will own a computer.
8	In fact, by 2050, printed books may have completely disappeared.
9	Students of the future will be using 'e-books', which so they can
10	download for themselves, from computers. Students who will be
11	spending more time working from at home, and a lot less time at school.
12	In fact, we'll all be spending more time at home. The future sounds great!

Vocabulary ▶ CB p.137

1 Word formation

1 Follow the instructions below. Write the words in your notebook.

1 Make verbs from these nouns:
a) *threat* b) *practice* c) *decision* d) *destruction*
e) *recycling*

2 Make nouns from these verbs:
a) *disappear* b) *inform* c) *save* d) *restrict*

3 Make adjectives from these verbs:
a) *poison* b) *destroy* c) *nature* d) *harm* e) *pollute*
f) *save*

2 Use the word in CAPITALS at the end of each sentence to form a word that fits in the gaps.

1 The World Wildlife Fund works to save animals from .... EXTINCT

2 There is a .... that the Arctic ice caps will melt. DANGEROUS

3 Factories produce .... gases. HARM

4 The sea is very .... in places. POLLUTE

5 We must not .... the countryside. DESTRUCTION

6 We should all take an interest in .... issues. ENVIRONMENT

7 People should .... their paper and glass. RECYCLING

8 We must keep the Earth .... for future generations to live in. SAVE

2 Phrasal verbs

Fill in the gaps with the correct form of a verb in the list. The particles are in *italics* to help you.

cut / give / keep / look / use / cut

1 We must .... *on* trying to save our planet.

2 We will soon .... *up* all the world's oil.

3 We should .... *down* on the amount of carbon dioxide we produce.

4 We must .... *after* the world's wildlife.

5 If we .... *down* all the rain forests, we will lose the 'lungs' of the world.

6 Power stations .... *off* dangerous gases.

3 Lexical cloze

Read the text and decide which answer A, B, C or D best fits each space. There is an example at the beginning (0).

| 0 | A for | B into | C over | D after |

FORESTS

In spite of all the warnings, we are still not looking **(0)** ..D.. our planet. Look what is happening to our forests. We are cutting them **(1)** .... at an alarming rate. If we keep **(2)** .... doing this, many animals and plants will **(3)** .... extinct. Rare **(4)** ...., such as the mountain gorilla, are already in **(5)** .... More will follow.

Forests are important for another reason, too. They help to slow the rate of global warming. Trees soak up gases **(6)** .... carbon dioxide, which are given **(7)** .... by power stations and factories. They **(8)** .... produce oxygen, and act as the lungs of the world.

It is clear that forests **(9)** .... a major contribution to the health of our planet. **(10)** .... it is a sad fact that very few governments have passed laws to protect them. Now, United Nations chiefs are studying the problem. They say that the best way to **(11)** .... forests is by educating the local people. These people often cut down forests because it is the only way they can **(12)** .... a living. But they do not wish to destroy their forests unnecessarily. If they are offered a different way to make money, hopefully they will **(13)** .... the forests alone.

1	A up	B in	C off	D down
2	A in	B up	C on	D at
3	A go	B get	C become	D result
4	A species	B tribes	C races	D specialities
5	A threat	B danger	C fact	D troubles
6	A as	B for	C like	D how
7	A off	B up	C out	D over
8	A too	B also	C nor	D either
9	A put	B make	C do	D play
10	A Although	B So	C In spite of	D Also
11	A safe	B arrange	C save	D aid
12	A do	B earn	C get	D have
13	A leave	B let	C allow	D permit

Writing: transactional letter

▶ CB p.139–140

1 Paragraph plan

Read the writing task on p.139 of your Coursebook. Then read the paragraph plan one student made before he wrote his answer.

1 Some points are irrelevant. Cross them out.
2 Some important items have been left out. Write them in.

Paragraph plan

Para. 1 (introduction)
- *Thank Ms Davies for her letter / for agreeing to come to the school.*

Para. 2
- *the date on which we want the talk*
- ....

Para. 3
- *how many students are planning to come*
- *a full description of the school*
- *how much will the talk cost?*
- ....

Para. 4 (conclusion)
- ....
- *any more information needed?*

2 Correct a sample answer

Now read the letter the student wrote. The student has not written a good introduction or conclusion. Write the letter in your notebook, including the missing items and adding an appropriate introduction and conclusion.

Dear Ms Davies,
Great! I'm so glad you're coming!
*   I wonder if you could possibly come on June 26th? Most of us will have finished our exams by then so we'll be able to give you our whole attention.*
*   I imagine there will be about 200 students all together. There's plenty of room in the school hall so that won't be a problem. Please let me know if you need any more information.*
*   Take care and see you soon!*
Yours sincerely,
...

3 Writing task

You are helping to organise a one-day conference on energy saving in your town. You have received a letter from someone volunteering to help. Read the letter you have received and the notes you have made. Then write a reply, giving all the necessary information.

Could you tell me where the conference is going to be held and when it will start and finish? I'm happy to help in any way. Maybe I could give out leaflets or something similar? By the way, I know there will be lots of experts there to give advice but will there be any special talks?
*   Yours faithfully*
*   Monika Simons*

My notes
- *conference to be held in Town Hall*
- *starts 08.00 and finishes 22.00.*
- *all volunteers to arrive by 07.30 if poss.*
- *people needed to put up tables and to clean up afterwards*
- *talk by member of Greenpeace at 14.30.*

Write a letter of between 120–180 words in an appropriate style. Do not write any addresses.

Remember to:

- read the exam question carefully.
- underline all the key points you have to cover in your letter.
- make a paragraph plan before you start.

Progress check 4

Grammar

1 Reported speech

Report the statements and questions, starting with the words given.

1 'I'm going on holiday tomorrow.'
Tim said (that) ....

2 'We've never been camping before.'
The boys said ....

3 'I'll ring you as soon as I can.'
Jason promised his girlfriend that ....

4 'We did most of our packing yesterday.'
They said ....

5 'I don't think your plane will leave on time.'
The stewardess told us that ....

6 'How much are the tickets, Jason?'
Pete asked Jason ....

7 'Have you remembered your passport, Pete?'
Jason asked ....

8 'Did you bring your mobile phone, Jason?'
Pete asked Jason ....

2 Find the mistake

Two sentences are correct. Tick them. <u>Underline</u> the mistakes in the other sentences and write them out correctly.

1 The expert warned us that we didn't play with the snake.
....

2 The boy admitted stealing the rabbit.
....

3 The teacher suggested us to go to the zoo.
....

4 My neighbour asked that I feed her cat.
....

5 My friends promised helping me look after the pony.
....

6 I suddenly realised that my dog had run away.
....

7 They advised me to not handle the lizard too much.
....

8 My family refused letting me buy a pet rat.
....

3 Impersonal statements

Put the words into the correct order to make sentences.

1 be castle haunted is said The to
The ....

2 bridge collapsed have is said The to
The bridge ....

3 Aromatherapy be said is relaxing to very
Aromatherapy ....

4 are be believed hair passionate People red to with
People with ....

5 are been crash have in injured known men the to Two
Two men ....

6 animals are endangered is It many said that
It ....

4 *have something done*

Fill in the gaps using the prompts in brackets.

1 Barbara went to the hairdresser's and ....
.... (have/her hair/cut)

2 Dad's going to the garage ....
tomorrow. (have/the car/service)

3 Which shop did you go to when you ....
.................? (have/ears/pierce)

4 If I were you, I'd .... the next time you go into town. (have/your eyes/test)

5 They've just .... by a firm of builders. (have/conservatory/build)

6 Last year, Sonya .... by a famous designer. (have/her wedding dress/make)

5 Future continuous or future perfect?

<u>Underline</u> the correct option in each pair.

1 I'm going on holiday so this time next week *I'll lie/I'll be lying* on the beach.

2 *Will you have got/Will you be getting* married by the time you're 30, do you think?

3 You can't borrow my computer this afternoon because *I'll have used/I'll be using* it myself.

4 *Will you still live/Will you still be living* in this town in ten years' time?

5 By the time I'm 80, I *may have become/may be becoming* a grandparent.

6 This time next year *I'll still learn/I'll still be learning* English.

Vocabulary

6 Words that go together

1 Match a word from Column A with a word from Column B.

A	B
1 build	a) clothes
2 carry	b) friends
3 endanger	c) a stick
4 make	d) the atmosphere
5 pollute	e) wildlife
6 wear	f) a house

2 Then fill in the gaps with the correct phrase from above. Be careful of tenses!

1 Smoke from the factories continues to ....

2 When we destroy rain forests we ....

3 Tom didn't know anyone when he arrived on the island but he soon ....

4 They .... on the beach and lived there for months.

5 In prehistoric times, people .... made of animal skins.

6 The old man is blind so he always ....

7 Phrasal verbs

Fill in the gaps with the correct verb from the list. Be careful of tenses!

carry / look / put / make / use / come

1 They've .... *up* a new housing estate in our town.

2 We should all .... *after* our health.

3 There's no milk so we'll have to .... *do* with black coffee.

4 I'm going to .... *on* having piano lessons for another year.

5 Linda .... *up* with a brilliant suggestion for our next holidays.

6 We've .... *up* all the wrapping paper – we'll have to buy some more.

8 Prepositions

Fill in the gaps with an appropriate preposition.

1 Anna comes .... the UK.

2 Did Paul take his mobile phone .... him?

3 Did you speak .... your girlfriend last night?

4 Sometimes Jason is friendly but .... other times he won't speak to anyone.

5 Sally was wearing a life jacket, which prevented her .... drowning.

6 The police suspected the man .... stealing some jewellery.

7 The teacher blamed us .... breaking the window.

8 My brother insists .... sitting in the front of the car.

9 Word formation

1 Complete the table.

Noun	Adjective	Verb
1	proud	xxx
2	3	save
harm	4	5 ....
threat	6	7 ....
8	9	live
10	pleasant	11 ....
danger	12	13 ....
14	varied/various	15 ....

2 Use the word in CAPITALS at the end of each sentence to form a noun or adjective that fits in the gap.

1 The sky looks .... I think it's going to snow. THREAT

2 Thank goodness you're .... – I've been really worried about you. SAVE

3 Boxing is a .... sport. DANGER

4 Smoking is .... to your health. HARM

5 Tropical rain forests contain an amazing .... of insects. VARY

6 You've just saved my ....! LIVE

Speaking ▶ CB p.143

Describing a photo

> ▶▶ *speaking strategy*
>
> When you are asked to speak about photos, listen carefully to what you are asked to do and make sure you don't forget the second part of the task. ◀◀

1 Read what the examiner says and <u>underline</u> the *two* tasks the candidate has to perform.

2 The candidate makes six grammar mistakes. Find them and write them in the spaces below.

Examiner: Compare and contrast these photos and say which event you'd prefer to be at.

Candidate: In this photo, the people look they live in Russia or somewhere near there. I think they're dressed in typical costumes for that area. There are lots of people dancing and playing instruments. I think it's probably a local festival, something typical for their region.

This other photo is very different. There are lots of people and they sit in a big park. It's a stage in the distance. Some of the people look like older – not just teenagers – so maybe it's an opera festival or something like that.

I think the people in both photos enjoy themselves but in different ways. I'd prefer to be at the Russian festival because it's completely different to anything I see before. I'd be interested to hear the music and see the dancing – and maybe even take part.

1 ....

2 ....

3 ....

4 ....

5 ....

6 ....

Reading ▶ CB pp.144–145

1 Definitions

Complete the definitions with words from the list.

slave / master / immigrant / founder / participant / expert

1 .... (n.) someone who takes part in an event

2 .... (n.) someone who starts an organisation

3 .... (n.) someone with special skills or knowledge

4 .... (n.) someone who is owned by another person and works for no pay

5 .... (n.) someone who owns another person or is in charge of them

6 .... (n.) someone who comes to live in another country permanently

2 Verb phrases

Fill in the gaps with the correct form of a verb from the list. The words in *italics* should help you.

dream / make / take / join / die / make

1 When slavery finished, the slaves .... *fun* of their masters.

2 The traditions the early slaves started have never .... *out*.

3 When West Indians settled in London, they .... *of* recreating their old carnivals.

4 Notting Hill is a London district which is .... *up of* many different cultural communities.

5 Tourists and visitors are all invited to .... *in* and dance.

6 These days, thousands of people .... *part in* the celebrations.

Grammar ▶ CB p.146, grammar file 21

1 *so* or *such (a)*?

Underline the correct option in each pair.

1 There was *so / such* loud music we couldn't hear each other speak.

2 It's *such / such* a famous festival that it attracts tourists from all over the world.

3 The organiser shouted *so / such* loudly that he lost his voice.

4 It was *such a / such* hot weather we didn't need sweaters.

5 There were *so / such* huge crowds that nobody could move.

6 The floats were *so / such* packed you couldn't see all the dancers.

7 The day passed *such / so* quickly that I didn't notice the time.

8 The procession made *such a / such* slow progress that it took an hour to go past me.

9 We got home *so / such* a late that everyone had gone to bed.

10 There were *such a / such* long queues that we gave up trying to buy tickets.

2 *too*

Rewrite the sentences, starting with the words given. Use the word *too*. Be careful with pronouns!

1 The festival was very important. He couldn't miss it.
   The festival was ....

2 The costumes were very hot. They couldn't wear them.
   The costumes were ....

3 The fireworks were very expensive. Tom couldn't buy them.
   The fireworks were ....

4 I was very late. I couldn't go to the concert.
   It was ....

5 The music was very slow. We couldn't dance to it.
   The music was ....

6 The streets were very crowded. Sarah couldn't walk along them.
   The streets were ....

7 The benches were very uncomfortable. They couldn't sit on them.
   The benches were ....

8 I was very busy. I didn't watch the parade.
   I was ....

3 *too, enough, very, so* or *such*?

Fill in the gaps with an appropriate word.

1 It was much .... crowded in the streets.

2 That's a .... beautiful costume. Where did you get it?

3 I didn't have .... money to buy any fireworks.

4 It was .... a good festival they've decided to hold it again next year.

5 The floats looked .... colourful that everyone clapped in appreciation.

6 It was far .... hot for us to stay in the sun.

7 The dancers passed .... quickly that I didn't have time to take a photo.

8 There was .... much traffic that the police had to close the road.

4 Find the mistake

Two sentences are correct. Tick them. Underline the mistakes in the other sentences and correct them.

1 The tickets weren't enough cheap. ....

2 We haven't got enough time to see everything. ....

3 I'm too old for wearing that fancy dress costume. ....

4 Are you enough warm? ....

5 The masks were too expensive to buy them. ....

6 The bench is too uncomfortable for the old man to sit. ....

7 If we wait enough long, we'll see the parade. ....

8 I'd like to watch the parade but I'm too busy to wait. ....

5 Extra word

Two sentences are correct. Tick them. The other sentences have one extra word that should not be there. Cross it out.

1 Tom was too tired for to come to the party.

2 It was such a lovely weather that we didn't need to wear our sweaters.

3 The streets were too crowded to drive along them.

4 I'll have a sandwich when I'm enough hungry.

5 It's much too early for us to go home.

6 I'm too sorry I missed the parade, but our car broke down.

7 I had such a fun that I never wanted the day to end.

8 I was so excited that I didn't notice the time.

6 Transformations

Complete the second sentence so that it has a similar meaning to the first, using the word given. Do not change the word given. Use between two and five words.

1 It was the most fabulous carnival I've ever been to.

   a

   I've never been to .... carnival before.

2 I was too short to see over the heads of the crowd.

   tall

   I wasn't .... over the heads of the crowd.

3 It's so hot we can't sit outside.

   us

   It's too hot .... outside.

4 I danced more than I've ever done before.

   much

   I've never .... before.

5 We were too excited to sleep.

   so

   We were .... couldn't sleep.

6 Gerald is so nervous that he can't sit still.

   too

   Gerald is .... still.

7 Sally can't buy fireworks because she is so young.

   old

   Sally isn't .... fireworks.

8 They danced so well they won a prize.

   such

   They were .... they won a prize.

9 The lights were so bright we couldn't look at them.

   for

   The lights were .... look at.

10 He didn't hire the costume because it was so expensive.

   him

   The costume was .... hire.

Vocabulary ▶ CB p.147

▌Verbs

Fill in the gaps with a verb from the list.

wrap / wish / have / celebrate / put up / decorated

1 On December 25th, people in Britain .... Christmas.

2 They .... paper decorations in the living room.

3 Most families have a Christmas tree, which is .... with lights and glass balls.

4 A lot of people .... parties at Christmas time.

5 It's customary for people to .... each other 'Happy Christmas'.

6 People usually .... their gifts in brightly coloured paper.

▌Word formation

Complete the table.

Verb	Noun	Adjective
decorate	1	2 ....
colour	colour	3 ....
xxx	4	famous
process	5	xxx
6	7	participating
8	9	celebratory
10	11	entertaining
xxx	romance	12 ....

3 Words that go together

1 Match a word from Column A with a word from Column B.

A

1 fancy
2 birthday
3 wrapping
4 firework
5 tourist

B

a) display
b) attraction
c) paper
d) dress
e) present

2 Fill in the gaps with an appropriate phrase.

1 Tom's 16 tomorrow. What shall we give him as a ....?

2 They're having a .... in that village – can you see the rockets in the sky?

3 Teresa's having a .... party and I'm going as Napoleon.

4 I bought some really pretty .... to go round Mum's present.

5 Mardi Gras in Brazil is very famous and has become a popular ....

4 Word formation

Use the word in CAPITALS underneath to form a word that fits in the space. There is an example at the beginning (0).

APRIL FAIR

The April fair in Seville started out as a regional, not a **(0)** ....*national*.... festival but it is now one of the most **(1)** .... festivals in Spain. During the festival, **(2)** .... put up hundreds of red and white or green and white tents. Triangular flags and other **(3)** .... are hung round the tents. At night, they are illuminated by thousands of lamps, which makes it a very **(4)** .... spectacle. The **(5)** .... begin at midnight and go on for a week. Girls and women wearing **(6)** .... flamenco dresses parade through the streets. There is horseback riding, bullfighting, singing and dancing and all sorts of other **(7)** .... During the day, floats full of flowers are driven through the streets in a noisy **(8)** .... Everywhere, there are couples dancing and guitarists playing music, both lively and **(9)** .... If you want to see the festival, make sure you book in advance or you'll find it **(10)** .... to find anywhere to stay.

0	NATION	**6**	TRADITION
1	FAME	**7**	ENTERTAIN
2	PARTICIPATE	**8**	PROCESS
3	DECORATE	**9**	ROMANCE
4	COLOUR	**10**	POSSIBLE
5	CELEBRATE		

Writing a story ▶ CB pp.149–150

Writing task

Read the writing task. <u>Underline</u> any important words.

Your teacher has asked you to write a story for the school's English language magazine. It must end with the following words:

'I knew this was going to be a special day,' Jason told himself.

Write your story in 120–180 words

Follow this procedure:

1 Think about a possible story. Note down some ideas.

2 Plan your story. Look at your notes and think about the order they might go in.

3 Write your story. Read the list of things to remember and look at the outline and useful phrases before you start.

4 Edit your story. Check for errors in grammar, spelling and punctuation.

Remember to:

• use a range of tenses. Use the past simple, the past continuous and the past perfect (but not the present perfect!) to describe finished events.

• use a range of descriptive vocabulary.

• make sure you use the right names or pronouns.

• use direct speech to make the story vivid.

Useful phrases

It all began when

In the beginning,

At first,

Then,

Later on

Meanwhile,

After a while,

In the end,

At last,

Suddenly,

The next minute,

Eventually,

Some time later,

Jason ....

....

....

....

....

....

....

....

....

....

....

....

....

....

.... *'I knew this was going to be a special day,' Jason told himself.*

Finish your story in an interesting way. Don't just write one sentence.

Divide your story into three or four paragraphs.

Use exactly the same words as in the exam question, and in the correct place.

18 Getting around

Speaking ▶ CB p.151

Conversation

Read the conversation and fill in the gaps with words or phrases from the list.

the word for / on / say that / prefer / in / chat / get / there's / in / on / by / on

Examiner: Here are your two photographs. They show people using different forms of transport. I'd like you to compare and contrast the photos and say why you think the people chose to travel this way.

Candidate A: OK. (1) .... this picture, I can see some people – they're getting (2) .... a coach. I think they're students because they're all quite young. They're all dressed in casual clothes and they've got bags – I'm afraid I don't know (3) .... these – (4) .... their backs. Maybe they're going (5) .... a group holiday. I like travelling (6) .... coach – you can just sit back and relax. And if you're in a group, you can all sing and (7) .... (8) .... the second picture, (9) .... an elderly couple sitting on a train. Maybe they're going to visit their grandchildren or something. I (10) .... the coach to the train because it's cheaper and it's more fun.

Examiner: OK, thank you. Now Katy, which of these forms of transport do you find most appealing?

Candidate B: I'm sorry, can you (11) .... again?

Examiner: Which type of transport do you find most appealing – do you like more?

Candidate B: Oh, I think the train is better because it's quicker and it's more comfortable. I always (12) .... sick on coaches!

Reading ▶ CB pp.152–153

1 Nouns

Fill in the gaps with an appropriate word from the list.

account / doubts / companion / fear / hike / landscape / trouble / trail / wilderness / view

1 Bill Bryson went for a .... through the Appalachians.

2 *A Walk in the Woods* is an .... of his journey.

3 The .... he followed was 2,200 miles long.

4 It went through a remote .... and woods.

5 He travelled with a ....

6 They had no .... finding their way.

7 If travellers have any .... about which way to go, there are signs to guide them.

8 Bryson's biggest .... was of bear attacks.

9 The walk was worth it because he learnt so much about the .... and about himself.

10 He enjoyed getting to a mountain top and admiring the .... from there.

2 Adjectives

1 Match a word from Column A with a word of a similar meaning from Column B.

A	B
1 agreeable	a) distant, lonely
2 congenial	b) funny
3 exaggerated	c) chatty, conversational
4 humorous	d) friendly
5 imaginable	e) uncommon
6 irrational	f) unreasonable
7 offended	g) made greater than it really is
8 rare	h) pleasant and relaxing
9 remote	i) possible to imagine
10 talkative	j) upset, angry

2 Fill in the gaps with an appropriate word from Column A.

1 Bryson crossed a .... mountain wilderness.

2 The book he wrote was extremely .... – it made me laugh a lot.

3 His companion was not very .... so they didn't talk very much.

4 He had a very .... relationship with his companion.

5 Bear attacks are very .... but they do happen sometimes.

6 Bryson's fear of bears was .... – in other words it was greater than normal.

7 Bears don't normally attack people so Bryson was being .... about them.

8 Bryson admitted that some aspects of his journey were not very ....

3 Prepositions/Prepositional phrases

Fill in the gaps with a suitable preposition.

1 The Appalachian trail is the longest footpath .... the world.

2 Bill Bryson travelled part of the trail .... foot.

3 He didn't meet many other people .... the trail.

4 He and his companion were not always .... sight of each other.

5 The fear that he would be attacked by a bear was always .... the back of his mind.

6 He found the journey was worth the effort .... the end.

Grammar ▶ CB p.154, grammar file 18

1 Present modals

Underline the correct option in each pair.

1 You *mustn't / needn't* go on the excursion if you don't want to. It's optional.

2 The policeman said we *mustn't / needn't* park here. It's not allowed.

3 Do I *have to / must* get a visa to go to the USA?

4 Christopher *doesn't need / needn't* a passport if he's not travelling abroad.

5 You *can / have to* take traveller's cheques if you like.

6 You *don't have to / shouldn't* ride a bike without a helmet.

7 You *don't need to / mustn't* book because there are plenty of rooms free in the hotel.

8 I don't think you *must / should* put so much in your suitcase. The handle will break!

2 Past modals

Fill in the gaps with *should* or *need* and the correct form of the underlined verbs.

1 You <u>drove</u> without a seatbelt, which was wrong of you. You ....*shouldn't have driven*.... without a seatbelt.

2 I <u>booked</u> the room in advance but the hotel was empty when I got there.

I .... the room in advance.

3 Steve didn't <u>tell</u> the customs officer about the whiskey in his suitcase, which was wrong of him.

He .... him about it.

4 Was it wrong of me to get on the bus before <u>paying</u>?

.... I .... before I got on the bus?

5 It wasn't necessary to <u>buy</u> a phone card (so I didn't buy one).

I .... a phone card.

6 Was it necessary for Paula to <u>catch</u> a later plane?

.... Paula .... a later plane?

7 We <u>queued</u> for tickets, but we found out later that there were plenty of them.

We .... for tickets.

8 They <u>made</u> a lot of noise on the coach, which was wrong of them.

They .... so much noise on the coach.

3 Find the mistake

Two sentences are correct. Tick them. <u>Underline</u> the mistakes in the other sentences and write the sentences correctly in your notebook.

1 We don't must book our tickets yet if we don't want to.
2 You ought to buy more traveller's cheques yesterday.
3 Tom needn't to buy a suitcase – I'll lend him mine.
4 Tom and Barbara didn't must get a taxi to the airport – their father took them instead.

5 We didn't have to wait long at the airport.
6 You ought have not gone away without telling your neighbours.
7 You can to sit next to me on the coach if you want to.
8 Sarah should have brought her swimming costume – I told her earlier that we were going to the beach.

4 *shouldn't, can* or *mustn't*

Complete these captions. Use a modal verb and a main verb in the correct form.

1 'You .... in the sea here!'

2 'You .... if you like!'

3 'You .... so fast!'

5 Error correction

Look carefully at each line. Four lines are correct. Tick them. The other lines contain one word which should not be there. <u>Underline</u> it.

HOLIDAY THRILLS

 0 Are you tired of studying? Do you feel you ought to <u>have</u>
00 take a holiday? If so, you might enjoy an adventure holiday. ✔
 1 This type of holiday is it becoming increasingly popular.
 2 In fact, over 100,000 adventure holidays have been sold this
 3 year alone! You don't always need have a lot of money to go
 4 on an adventure holiday. You can to stay in your own country
 5 and take the part in all sorts of activities. However, if you want
 6 to enjoy some of the most thrilling holidays, you need it to go
 7 abroad. You could be dive with Great White sharks, for
 8 example, or visit the Arctic Circle and meet the Inuit. While
 9 these holidays are certainly exciting, you should ever remember
10 not to take unnecessary risks. Jason North ended up in hospital
11 after falling from a mountain in Borneo. 'I ought to have been
12 taken more care and had followed the guide more closely,' he
13 admitted later. Clare and Paul Clark were needed major surgery
14 after a rhino attacked them in southern Nepal. 'We shouldn't had
15 have left the trail,' they said later. 'We had a lucky escape.'

Vocabulary ▶ CB p.155

1 Word sets: travel

Look at the words in the box. Put them under the correct heading. Write the table in your notebook.

> visa   guide   clerk   boarding card   travel agent
> tourist   pedestrian   credit card   passenger
> traveller's cheques   sightseer   passport   driving licence

People	Items to take / pack

Words that go together

Put the words in the box into the appropriate list. Some words will fit in more than one list.

> a bicycle   a bus   a boat   a car   a train
> a taxi   a ferry   a plane   a coach   a motorcycle

1 You can drive ...*a bus, a car, a train, a taxi, a coach*.......
2 You can get on / get off a ....
3 You can get into / get out of a ....
4 You can board ....
5 You can catch ....
6 You can ride ....
7 You can fly in ....
8 You can sail in ....

Prepositions

Fill in the gaps with the correct preposition from the list.

at / by / with / on / on / in / off / on

1 I've never been .... a cruise.
2 Jessica came .... her own car.
3 I prefer travelling .... train.
4 Sam has gone .... a trip.
5 Did you come all this way .... foot?
6 I spent my holidays .... friends.
7 Their plane is going to land .... Heathrow Airport.
8 What time does our plane take ....?

4 Travel

Fill in the gaps with an appropriate word.

1 Oh no! We're going to .... our bus!
2 I'm going to the travel .... to get some holiday brochures.
3 If we want to see the island, why don't we .... a car for two weeks?
4 What time will we .... at our destination?
5 The check-in clerk says there's a two-hour .... to our flight because of fog.
6 I love sitting in the airport and watching the planes take off and ....

5 Open cloze

Read the text and think of the word that best fits each space. Use only one word in each space. There is an example at the beginning (0).

KNOW YOUR RIGHTS

Before going **(0)** .....*on*........ holiday, it's a good **(1)** .... to find out what your legal rights are. Imagine, **(2)** .... example, that you **(3)** .... at the airport and go straight to the check-in **(4)** .... The staff inform you that your plane has a technical problem and there will be a six-hour **(5)** .... Or perhaps you set **(6)** .... on a package tour. The plane is overbooked and it takes **(7)** .... without you. If this happens, go straight to your tour operator or travel **(8)** .... You will get a refund.

Now, imagine you book a hotel **(9)** .... with a sea view. When you **(10)** .... to the hotel, you find the sea is three kilometres away. Or maybe you discover that the luxury hotel you read about in the travel **(11)** .... has not been built yet! Don't despair. The law will protect you in most countries.

When you travel, do take traveller's **(12)** .... with you – don't take cash or credit **(13)** ....! Hotels are not obliged to help if your cash is stolen.

If this advice has **(14)** .... you feel anxious, forget it. You will probably have nothing to complain **(15)** .... while you are away – except that you have to come home!

Writing an article ► CB pp.157–158

Writing task

Read the writing task. <u>Underline</u> any important words.

> **Write an article for a student magazine about a city you have visited recently and say why it impressed you.**
>
> **Write your article in 120–180 words.**

Follow this procedure:

1. think about the question. Make notes:
   a) about the city
   b) giving the reasons why it impressed you.
2. Plan your article. Look at your notes and think about the order they might go in.
3. Write your article. Read the list of things to remember and look at the outline and useful phrases before you start.
4. Edit your article. Check for errors in grammar, spelling and punctuation.

Remember to:

- make your article lively and interesting. Imagine your reader is in the room with you!
- use the right style; don't use very formal language, but don't be too casual, either.

Useful phrases

You could never get bored in (name of city) because

Why is (name of city) so popular with tourists? It's probably because

Everywhere you go, you see

There is/there are

During the day/At night,

If you like …, go to (name of city). I guarantee you won't be disappointed.

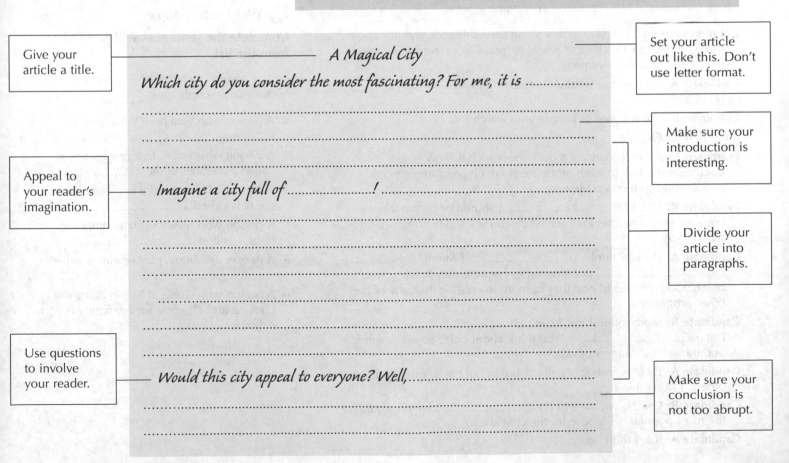

Give your article a title.

Set your article out like this. Don't use letter format.

A Magical City

Which city do you consider the most fascinating? For me, it is ....

Make sure your introduction is interesting.

Appeal to your reader's imagination.

Imagine a city full of ....! ....

Divide your article into paragraphs.

Use questions to involve your reader.

Would this city appeal to everyone? Well,.................

Make sure your conclusion is not too abrupt.

19 The age of TV

Speaking ▶ CB p.159

Definitions

Complete the definitions with words from the list.

cartoon / chat show / documentary / quiz / science fiction / wildlife

1 .... (n.) a serious TV programme that gives you information and facts

2 .... (adj.) depicting life in the future

3 .... (n.) a show in which famous people are interviewed

4 .... (n.) a competition where people answer questions and may win prizes

5 .... (n.) a film made using characters that are drawn, not real

6 .... (n.) animals and nature

Collaborative task

Fill in the gaps with words from the list.

agree / choose / like / mean / so / think / what

Examiner: Now I'd like you to talk about something together for about three minutes. A TV channel wants to increase its teenage viewing figures for Saturday evenings.

Candidate A: Excuse me, what does 'viewing figures' (1) ....?

Examiner: It's the number of people who watch TV.

Candidate A: Oh, OK.

Examiner: They can broadcast a quiz show, a chat show or a documentary. Talk to each other about which programme would appeal most to teenage viewers.

Candidate B: OK. I (2) .... it should be a chat show because young people love seeing celebrities and hearing what they have to say.

Candidate A: Do you think (3) ....? Mmm, I (4) .... documentaries because they teach you so much about the world and they're more interesting than any of the other programmes.

Candidate B: More interesting? I can't (5) ...., I'm sorry. But (6) .... do you think about quiz shows? Are they popular with teenagers or not?

Candidate A: They're probably quite popular, but not as interesting as the others, I don't think.

Candidate B: OK. So we have to (7) .... which would be the most popular. I suppose it's the chat show?

Candidate A: Yes, I think so.

Reading ▶ CB pp.160–161

1 Word sets: people

Complete the sentences with a word from the list.

critic / viewer / character / audience / housewife / scriptwriter

1 A person who watches TV is called a ....

2 A person who listens to a programme is called a member of the ....

3 A person who writes the words the actors speak is called a ....

4 A person who reviews programmes or films is called a ....

5 A person in a book, play or film is called a ....

6 A person who works at home, doing the cooking and cleaning for her family is called a ....

2 Verbs

Fill in the gaps with the correct form of a verb from the list.

predict / analyse / gossip / copy / concentrate / broadcast / capture / create

1 My favourite soap is .... on Mondays, Wednesdays and Fridays.

2 Soap opera is a type of programme that has .... the imagination of the whole world.

3 Scriptwriters .... complicated plots centred on the same family or community.

4 The plot is easy to follow so you don't have to .... very hard to understand it.

5 Some viewers enjoy .... about soap operas as much as watching them.

6 Viewers like to .... what will happen in the next episode of the soap.

7 Viewers also like to .... the behaviour and motives of the characters in the episode they have just watched.

8 Sometimes fans try to .... their favourite characters and even dress and speak in the same way they do.

3 Verbs + prepositions

Fill in the gaps with a verb from the list. The prepositions are in *italics*, to help you.

addicted / based / find / identify / succeeded / tune

1 Many viewers .... *with* characters in soap operas.

2 Soap operas have .... *in* winning large audiences round the world.

3 My sister is .... *to* soap operas – she can't stop watching them!

4 The soap opera I watch is .... *on* life in a small village.

5 Millions of viewers .... *in* to their favourite serial every week.

6 After a cliff-hanger, everyone is desperate to .... *out* what will happen next.

4 True or false?

Read these sentences and decide if they are true (T) or false (F). Check your answers by looking at the text in your Coursebook on pp.160–161.

1 The first soap operas were radio programmes. ....

2 Soap operas were originally made by soap powder manufacturers. ....

3 They often have more than one storyline. ....

4 Viewers of soap operas never confuse real life and fiction. ....

5 Each episode of a soap opera ends with a cliff-hanger. ....

6 Everyone agrees that soaps are good for you. ....

Grammar

▶ CB p.162, grammar file 10

1 *-ing* form or infinitive?

Underline the correct option in each pair.

1 It's good for you *to spend / spending* time relaxing.

2 That soap opera is not worth *to watch / watching*.

3 It was impossible *to meet / meeting* the actors because they were busy.

4 I can't help *to read / reading* what's going to happen next in the TV guide.

5 *To try / Trying* to get tickets for the show is pointless.

6 It was clever of you *to guess / guessing* the ending of the film.

7 *To laze / Lazing* in front of the TV all day is not very healthy.

8 My new video camera is great but it's difficult *to operate / operating*.

2 *-ing* forms as subject

Combine the sentences, starting with an *-ing* form.

1 You play computer games all the time. That is bad for your eyes.

Playing ....

....

2 They bought a second-hand TV. That was a big mistake.

....

3 He took part in a TV quiz show. That was the most embarrassing thing he had ever done.

....

....

4 They saw the film. It wasn't as good as reading the book.

....

5 She watched a horror film alone. It was really scary.

....

6 They made their own video. It was great fun.

....

3 Phrases and adjectives

Fill in the gaps with the correct form of the verb in brackets.

1 It's a waste of time .... (watch) cartoons all day.

2 It was nice of you .... (let) me watch your TV.

3 I was glad .... (hear) that my favourite film was being shown again.

4 It was fun .... (meet) my favourite actor.

5 .... (miss) the latest episode of the soap opera was a disaster for me!

6 I was shocked .... (hear) that the series was going to finish.

7 It was hard for my brother .... (give up) watching TV.

8 It's easy .... (operate) our new video machine.

4 Transformations

Complete the second sentence so that it has a similar meaning to the first, using the word given. Do not change the word given. Use between two and five words.

1 Copying characters from soap operas is silly. **to**
It's .... characters from soap operas.

2 You broke the video, which was careless. **of**
It was .... the video.

3 Seeing my favourite character in real life was a shock. **shocked**
I was .... my favourite character in real life.

4 Looking at a screen all day is not good for your health. **bad**
It's .... at a screen all day.

5 I find it difficult not to laugh at that comedian. **help**
I .... at that comedian.

6 There's no point hiring a video because the machine is broken. **use**
It .... a video because the machine is broken.

7 The music was very loud so he couldn't hear the actors. **impossible**
The music was very loud so it was .... the actors.

8 Watching that play was pointless. **waste**
It was .... that play.

9 Introducing me to the actors was kind of you. **kind**
It was .... me to the actors.

10 It's pointless trying to repair the TV. **worth**
It's .... to repair the TV.

Vocabulary ▶ CB p.163

1 Word formation

1 Follow the instructions. Write the words in your notebook.

1 Make nouns from these verbs:
a) *entertain*   b) *enjoy*   c) *believe*   d) *vary*

2 Make nouns from these adjectives:
a) *popular*   b) *amazing*   c) *responsible*
d) *difficult*   e) *able*

3 Make adjectives from these nouns:
a) *scare*   b) *fiction*   c) *boredom*
d) *culture*   e) *tragedy*

2 Fill in the gaps with an appropriate word.

1 The horror film we watched last night was really ....

2 I enjoy quiz programmes but I find soap operas really ....

3 I had .... following the plot of that film.

4 The ending to *Romeo and Juliet* is really .... – I cried when I saw it!

5 The play wasn't based on fact; it was entirely ....

2 Film words

Fill in the gaps with an appropriate word from the list.

cast / character / hero / script / channel / villain

1 James Bond is the .... of the Ian Fleming spy novels.

2 The producer congratulated the .... on their performances.

3 Dustin Hoffman once played a .... called Mrs Doubtfire.

4 In old films, the bad guy or .... always wore a black hat.

5 Julia Roberts has been sent a .... to read for a new film.

6 I'll look in the TV guide and check which .... the film is on.

3 Prepositions

Underline the correct word in each pair.

1 There's nothing *in / on* TV tonight.

2 *Planet of the Apes* is set *on / in* the future.

3 Penelope Cruz is famous *in / for* playing romantic leads.

4 *Jurassic Park* is based *in / on* a novel by Michael Crichton.

5 People watch soaps at least once a week, *in / on* average.

6 They wrote a play about Eva Peron and then they put it *in / on* screen.

4 Lexical cloze

Read the text and decide which answer A, B, C or D best fits each space.
There is an example at the beginning (0).

0 **A** onlookers   **B** spectators   **C** seers   **D** viewers

REALITY TV

Every day, millions of (**0**) ..*D*.. round the world (**1**) .... into programmes like *Big Brother*. It seems that (**2**) .... just can't get enough of them. But why do so many of us want to (**3**) .... these programmes? The (**4**) .... who star in these 'reality' TV shows are becoming as familiar (**5**) .... our own families. So are these new programmes very different from soap (**6**) ....? In the (**7**) ...., it seems, they are not. Both sorts of shows have good guys or heroes, and bad guys or (**8**) ...., just like in the soaps. They can both help us understand human behaviour and each daily or weekly (**9**) .... usually ends with a (**10**) .... so we have to (**11**) .... on the next time to check what has happened. But why do we want to see ordinary people on (**12**) ....? Are we so (**13**) .... to TV that we just can't turn it (**14**) .... any longer? Or are our own lives really (**15**) .... boring that we can only experience relationships through other people on the 'box'?

1	**A** switch	**B** tune	**C** channel	**D** plug
2	**A** audiences	**B** hearers	**C** listeners	**D** customers
3	**A** look	**B** watch	**C** stare	**D** notice
4	**A** persons	**B** players	**C** people	**D** actors
5	**A** than	**B** so	**C** as	**D** that
6	**A** operas	**B** dramas	**C** shows	**D** plays
7	**A** end	**B** final	**C** last	**D** least
8	**A** critics	**B** villains	**C** casts	**D** saints
9	**A** series	**B** serial	**C** episode	**D** part
10	**A** serial	**B** drama	**C** cliff-hanger	**D** series
11	**A** switch	**B** go	**C** take	**D** put
12	**A** glass	**B** channel	**C** stage	**D** screen
13	**A** keen	**B** addicted	**C** fond	**D** enthusiastic
14	**A** down	**B** out	**C** off	**D** on
15	**A** rather	**B** such	**C** so	**D** most

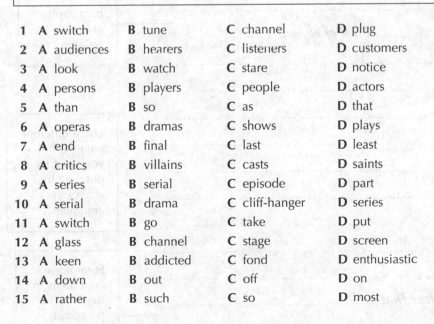

Writing a composition ▶ CB pp.165–166

Writing task
Read the writing task. <u>Underline</u> the important words.

> **You have been discussing TV programmes and soap operas in class. Your teacher has asked you to write a composition, giving your opinion on the following statement.**
>
> *We get all the information we need from television and newspapers – books are no longer necessary.*
>
> **Write your composition in 120–180 words.**

Follow this procedure:

1 Think about the question. Make notes.

2 Plan your composition. Look at your notes and think about the order they might go in.

3 Write your composition. Look at the outline and useful phrases before you start.

4 Edit your composition. Check for errors in grammar, spelling and punctuation.

Useful phrases

giving opinions	sequencing ideas	adding more ideas	putting the other side of the argument	expressing contrast	summing up
As far as I'm concerned	In the first place, Secondly, Finally	Also, Added to this, Furthermore, Moreover	On the other hand	However, In spite of this, Nevertheless, Although	In conclusion

Develop your introduction. Don't just write one sentence.

Make your opinion clear to the reader all through your composition.

Give examples to back up your arguments.

Explain your arguments in detail.

Use linking expressions to connect sentences and paragraphs.

Nowadays most of us own a television or a radio, so we can get the latest news and entertainment by just turning on our sets. It seems that people read hardly anything these days, except for newspapers. Does it matter?

In my opinion,..
.... *First of all,* ....
....

This is because ....
In the second place, ...
....
....

However, ...
....
....

To sum up, it seems clear that ....
....
....

You can refer to the exam question but do not copy it word for word.

Use one paragraph to give your opinion.

Use a different paragraph if you want to put the other side of the argument.

Summarise your ideas in the final paragraph and add a comment.

Speaking ▶ CB p.167

Conversation

Read the conversation below. There is a mistake in each of the phrases in *italics*. Find the mistakes and write the phrases again correctly in the space below.

Examiner: Do students get too much homework these days?

Candidate A: **(1)** *I think it depend* which school you go to. **(2)** *I mean, by example,* in my school our teachers are very thoughtful – they never give us homework at weekends. I think that's a good idea.

Candidate B: Yes, **(3)** *but in the other hand,* I think students have to study at home if they want to pass exams. I think when you're 16 or 17 you need to study every night. For me, it's normal.

…

Examiner: Should students be allowed to leave school when they're 14?

Candidate B: **(4)** *No, I don't think it.* **(5)** *I don't understand it why* anyone would want to do that. **(6)** *I think is it very important* to have a good education.

Candidate A: Mmm, yes. **(7)** *I think it's right.*

…

Examiner: Should the school holidays be longer?

Candidate A: Definitely! I think students and teachers both need more time to relax. **(8)** *What are you think?*

Candidate B: **(9)** *Yes, you've right.*

1 ....
2 ....
3 ....

4 ....
5 ....
6 ....
7 ....

8 ....
9 ....

Reading ▶ CB pp.168–169

1 Words that go together

1 Match a word from Column A with a word or phrase from Column B.

A	B
1 clear	a) tired, stressed
2 do	b) a question, a problem
3 get	c) notes, sure
4 give (someone)	d) television, a video
5 make	e) hours, time
6 spend, waste	f) your best
7 tackle	g) your head, your mind
8 watch	h) advice

2 Fill in the gaps with an appropriate verb. Be careful of tenses.

1 I never .... television on weekdays.

2 My neighbour .... me some good advice.

3 I'm going for a short walk to .... my head.

4 Before you go out, ... sure you lock the door.

5 Don't worry if you can't answer all the questions – just .... your best.

6 When you .... tired of watching that football match, we can play a game.

2 Verbs

Fill in the gaps with a verb from the list.

*avoid / concentrate / glance / ignore /
panic / revise / tackle / waste*

1 A lot of people lose their heads and
.... when they have to do
an exam.

2 Give yourself plenty of time to
.... your work before an
exam.

3 You should .... late nights if
you have an exam the next day.

4 Don't .... too much time
worrying about the exam.

5 Never .... a question
without making notes first.

6 In the exam room, try to ....
the people sitting next to you.

7 You may find it useful to ....
through your notes the night before an
exam.

8 A cup of black coffee sometimes helps you
to ....

3 Verbs + prepositions

**Fill in the gaps with an appropriate
preposition. The verbs in *italics* will help
you to choose.**

1 The night before an exam you can relax
by *going* .... with friends.

2 You shouldn't *stay* .... too late if
you have an exam the next day.

3 You don't have to *give* ....
everything just because you have exams.

4 *Talk* problems .... with your friends
or parents.

5 *Put* .... a CD before you go to
sleep and it will help you to relax.

6 The best way to *cope* .... stress is
to take time off.

7 Don't let your friends *put* you ....
studying.

8 Helena doesn't *believe* .... doing
all her revision at the last minute.

Grammar ▶ CB p.170, grammar file 19

1 Mixed modals

Match a sentence from Column A with a sentence from Column B.

A

1 The ground is wet.

2 Sarah looks fed up.

3 My friend says he's got a date
with actress Sandra Bullock.

4 Stella's got a new computer.

5 Paul's not answering the phone.

6 Bill's at the doctor's.

B

a) Her dad might have bought
it for her.

b) He must be out.

c) She can't have passed her test.

d) He must be feeling ill.

e) It must have been raining.

f) He must be joking!

2 Past modals

Fill in the gaps with the correct form of the verbs in brackets.

1 **A:** Tina looked delighted when she got her exam results.
   B: Good. She .... (must/pass) them.

2 **A:** The headmaster was furious with the boys.
   B: They .... (must/fight) when he saw them.

3 **A:** Peter broke a bottle in the chemistry lab today.
   B: Well he .... (couldn't/concentrate) at
   the time.

4 **A:** Sarah wasn't in school this morning.
   B: She .... (might/go) to the dentist's.

5 **A:** I had three exams yesterday.
   B: Heavens! You .... (must/be) exhausted by
   the time you got home.

6 **A:** Clare can't find her wallet. It's not in her bag.
   B: She .... (might/leave) it in school.

7 **A:** I saw Tom at the bus stop. Where do you suppose he was going?
   B: I don't know. He .... (couldn't/go)
   to school because it's closed today.

8 **A:** Who is that man? He isn't a teacher.
   B: I don't know. He .... (might/come) to see
   the headmaster.

3 Find the mistake

Two sentences are correct. Tick them. Underline the mistakes in the other sentences and correct them.

1 Vicky is revising. She can have an exam tomorrow.
....

2 You've written the wrong answer. You can't read the question very carefully. ....

3 That man mustn't be an examiner. He's not old enough. ....

4 Tim's still in his bedroom. He might revise for his test.
....

5 Paul fell off his bike. He couldn't have been looking where he was going. ....

6 Clare's not at home. She must go out. ....

7 Your watch isn't here. You must lose it. ....

8 Miss Smith might take the class today. Our usual teacher isn't here. ....

9 Harry came last in the end of term test. He couldn't do much work during the term. ....

10 You look pale – you must work too hard recently.
....

4 What are they saying?

Look at the pictures and complete the captions. Use the verbs in brackets to help you.

1 'He must .... to drive!' (forget)

2 'Gwen can't .... revision!' (do)

5 Open cloze

Read the text and think of the word that best fits each space. Use only one word in each space. There is an example at the beginning (0).

ARE OUR STUDENTS GETTING CLEVERER?

Children in the UK (0) ....*are*........ getting better exam results than at (1) .... time in the past. Critics think that examination standards (2) .... be falling and that exam papers must (3) .... getting easier. They say that children couldn't (4) .... improved so much in (5) .... a short time. The change in the exam syllabus (6) ...., perhaps, explain the better results. It is also true that 18-year-olds now take 'modules' or 'mini exams' in various subjects every few months instead (7) .... taking one big final exam. Some critics believe that this new system (8) .... make exams easier.

However, both teachers (9) .... their students strongly disagree (10) .... this suggestion. They believe that good exam results are the result of pure hard work and (11) .... else. 'We've (12) .... to work really hard (13) .... get good grades,' one student complained, 'and now people say we don't deserve them. It's not fair.' Nobody (14) .... deny that today's teenagers work extremely hard for their success. So perhaps adults need (15) .... congratulate young people more often instead of criticising them all the time.

3 'Susan .... her exams!' (pass)

4 'He .... someone on his mobile phone to get the answers!' (phone)

Vocabulary ▶ CB p.171

1 Choosing the right word

Complete the sentences with the correct word. Use each word once only.

> pass   take   fail   succeed

1 Don't worry. If you .... your exams, you can take them again.

2 If I want to .... in my career, I'll have to work a bit harder!

3 My brother is going to .... his driving text tomorrow but I don't think he'll ....!

> do   make   get   give

4 Try not to .... so many mistakes this time!

5 The teacher says she's going to .... us a test tomorrow.

6 I can't go out tonight – I've got to .... some revision.

7 I hope I .... good grades in my exams!

> class   topic   subject   course

8 All the students arrived late for .... this morning.

9 What is your favourite .... at school, English or Maths?

10 I'm going on a six-week .... in scuba-diving.

11 What .... are we discussing in our Sociology class today?

> teacher   professor   instructor

12 Mr Jones is a driving ....

13 Barbara has been teaching English Literature at the university for years and now she's been made a ....

14 My sister goes to secondary school and she loves her Maths ....

2 Phrasal verbs

Fill in the gaps with an appropriate preposition. The verbs are in *italics* to help you.

1 My dad *told* me .... because I got a bad report from school.

2 Kevin broke the leg off his desk but the teacher *let* him .... with a warning.

3 Let's *look* John's address .... on the computer.

4 I didn't know the right answer to the question so I *made* something ....

5 I can't *work* .... how to do this Chemistry experiment.

6 Quick! *Rub* that mistake .... before the teacher sees it!

3 Word formation

Use the word in CAPITALS underneath to form a word that fits in the space. There is an example at the beginning (0).

LET TV SWITCH ON YOUR BRAIN!

Are you hoping to become a famous (0) .*politician*..? Or maybe your talents are (1) .... or (2) .... rather than practical? Whatever career you have in mind, you may be (3) .... to hear that watching TV may make you more (4) .... in your exams!

Would you like to know more? Well, (5) .... gave two groups of students the same intelligence test. Those who sat (6) .... in front of the 'box' for half an hour before the test did better than those who didn't. Does that sound (7) ....? Well, it's actually true. It seems that watching TV causes certain (8) .... changes in your brain – it warms your brain up, much as an athlete warms up before a race. However, researchers warn that there are really no short cuts to exam success. Without hard work and plenty of (9) ...., all your efforts will end in (10) .... You don't get anything, it seems, without hard work.

---

0 POLITICS	**6** LAZY
1 ART	**7** CREDIBLE
2 MUSIC	**8** CHEMIST
3 SURPRISE	**9** REVISE
4 SUCCESS	**10** FAIL
5 PSYCHOLOGY	

Writing a report ▶ CB pp.173–174

Writing task

Read the writing task. <u>Underline</u> any important words.

> Your English teacher has asked for your suggestions on the type of improvements needed to make the school a more welcoming place for students, staff and visitors.
>
> Write your report in 120–180 words.

Follow this procedure:

1 Think about the question. Make notes about the improvements you want to suggest.

2 Plan your report. Look at your notes and think about the order they might go in.

3 Write your report. Look at the outline and the useful language in it before you start.

4 Edit your report. Check for errors in grammar, spelling and punctuation.

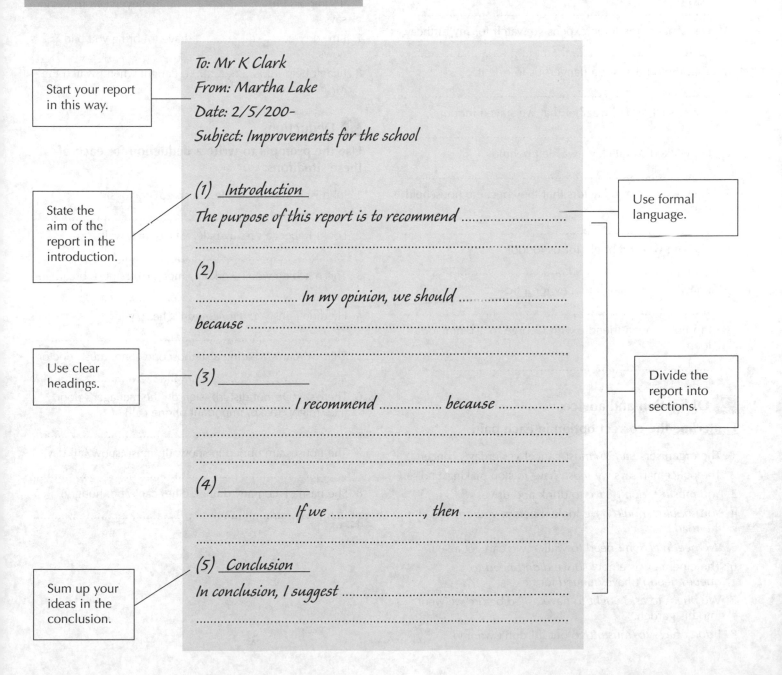

Start your report in this way.

State the aim of the report in the introduction.

Use clear headings.

Sum up your ideas in the conclusion.

To: Mr K Clark
From: Martha Lake
Date: 2/5/200-
Subject: Improvements for the school

(1) Introduction
The purpose of this report is to recommend ....

....

(2) _____

.... In my opinion, we should ....

because ....

....

(3) _____

.... I recommend .... because ....

....

....

(4) _____

.... If we ...., then ....

....

(5) Conclusion
In conclusion, I suggest ....

....

Use formal language.

Divide the report into sections.

Progress check 5

Grammar

1 Cause and result

Two sentences are correct. Tick them. <u>Underline</u> the mistakes in the other sentences and write the sentences correctly.

1 I'm not enough rich to buy a car.

....

2 He's too young for watch a horror movie.

....

3 Dad bought me a too expensive watch for my birthday.

....

4 That motorbike is too dangerous to ride it.

....

5 It was such a bad weather that we stayed indoors.

....

6 He walked so quickly I was left behind.

....

7 They were so good actors that they became household names.

....

8 The sun was too bright for us to look.

....

9 I haven't got enough money for a ticket.

....

10 I'm not enough friendly with George to ask him for a loan.

....

2 Obligation and advice

<u>Underline</u> the correct option in each pair.

1 The organisers *had to / must* cancel yesterday's concert.

2 The policeman says we *must / have to* stop making a noise.

3 You *mustn't / don't have to* drink and drive.

4 You *should / should have* looked before you crossed the road.

5 We *needn't / don't need to* walk – we can get a taxi.

6 The cinema was empty so we *didn't need to queue / needn't have queued* for tickets.

7 We *ought to ask / ought to have asked* before we went into his garden.

8 I *don't have to / mustn't* go out if I don't want to.

3 *-ing* forms and infinitives

Fill in the gaps using the verbs in brackets.

1 .... (ski) can be quite a dangerous sport.

2 It's a waste of time .... (buy) that video – it's useless.

3 I was astonished .... (hear) the news.

4 .... (act) in a play is great fun.

5 It's bad for you .... (stare) at a computer screen all day.

6 It's impossible .... (believe) a word Kevin says.

7 I'm sorry .... (have to) bring you bad news.

8 I can't help .... (laugh) when I watch the *Mr Bean* video.

4 Deductions

Use the prompts to write a deduction for each of these situations.

1 John isn't in school. (He / must / go / doctor's)

....

2 Look! Rebecca's really pale. (She / can't / well)

....

3 This machine won't work any more. (You / must / break / it!)

....

4 He didn't answer. (He / couldn't / hear / you)

....

5 That woman's wearing a stethoscope. (She / must / doctor)

....

6 There's a 'Do not disturb' sign on the manager's door. (He / might / make / important phone call)

....

7 The houses are buried in snow. (It / must / snow / all day)

....

8 She hasn't eaten any dinner. (She / can't / be / hungry)

....

Vocabulary

5 Words that go together

1 Match a word from Column A with a word from Column B.

A	B
1 celebrate	a) a war
2 decorate	b) taxes
3 take	c) an important event
4 fight	d) a new law
5 raise	e) a test
6 approve	f) a room

2 Fill in the gaps with phrases from above. Be careful of tenses!

1 The government have just ....
.... banning smoking in all public places.

2 Before you can drive a car you must ....
....

3 We bought some paint and wallpaper because we want to .... in our house.

4 The soldiers were called up to ....
.... against terrorism.

5 People often have a party when they want to
....

6 The President wants to ....
.... to pay for a better health service.

6 Phrasal verbs

Fill in the gaps with the correct verb from the list.

dress / ended / make / put / set / work

1 I offered to .... my friend *up* overnight.

2 We intended to go to the cinema but we .... *up* in the disco.

3 At carnival time, we usually ....
ourselves *up* in fancy dress costumes.

4 What time should we .... *off* for the airport?

5 I'll have to .... *up* an excuse for missing class.

6 I can't .... *out* the answer to this problem.

7 Prepositions

<u>Underline</u> the correct word in each pair.

1 I've just been *at/on* an excursion.

2 Our galaxy is made up *of/from* many stars.

3 The stars and planets move *among/through* space.

4 One *from/of* my friends is getting married next year.

5 What time did you arrive *on/at* the station?

6 I came here *by/on* foot.

7 The film director, Hitchcock, is famous *in/for* horror films.

8 There's nothing *in/on* TV tonight.

8 Word formation

1 Complete the table.

Noun	Adjective	Adverb
attraction	1	2 ....
success	3	4 ....
fame	5	6 ....
7	elegant	8 ....
9	good	10 ....
xxx	bad	11 ....
tradition	12	13 ....
fashion	14	15 ....
trend	16	17 ....
18	19	possibly

2 Use the word in CAPITALS at the end of each sentence to form a word that fits in the gap.

1 You speak English very .... GOOD

2 Body painting is quite .... at the moment. FASHION

3 Victoria Beckham became .... when she joined the Spice Girls. FAME

4 ...., British people eat turkey at Christmas. TRADITION

5 Her boyfriend wears really .... clothes. TREND

6 Is there any .... of getting tickets for the concert? POSSIBLE

Answer Key

1 One world

Speaking ▶ p.2

1.1 1 I'd like to go to university and study law.
2 I've/I have got three older brothers and one sister.
3 I live in a block of flats near the town centre.
4 I love my town because there's/there is so much to do.
5 I share a room with my older sister.
6 I often meet my friends in town on Saturdays.
7 I live near my school so I can walk there every morning.
8 I like listening to music in my free time.

1.2 a) 7 b) 5 c) 8 d) 1 e) 3 f) 6 g) 2 h) 4

2.1 1 d) 2 e) 3 g) 4 b) 5 h) 6 f) 7 a) 8 c)

2.2 1 So do I 2 can mine 3 can I 4 Nor/Neither does my mum. 5 Nor/Neither have we.
6 So does mine.

Reading ▶ p.3

1 1 native speakers 2 official 3 multi-lingual environment 4 cultural awareness 5 strategies
6 skills 7 context 8 Last but not least

2.2 1 animal 2 tree 3 knife 4 injury

3 1 C 2 D 3 A 4 B

4 1 at, in 2 in 3 into 4 in 5 in 6 down

Grammar ▶ p.4

1 1 's/is having 2 usually walks 3 are thinking
4 do you think 5 's/is working 6 take 7 look
8 'm looking/am looking 9 don't go out, usually stay
10 Does this book belong

2 1 Are you having a good time in Britain?
2 Which hotel are you staying at?
3 Do you like the way of life over there?
4 What special things do you want to see while you are there?
5 Do English people speak very quickly?
6 Is the sun shining at the moment or is it raining?
7 What time do people normally have dinner over there?
8 Do you go sightseeing every day?

3 1 We rarely watch TV in the evenings.
2 My brother and I don't often fight.
3 I sometimes go shopping in the town centre at weekends.
4 Do you usually go out with your friends in the evenings?
5 (Now and again) My mum drives my sister to the beach (now and again).
6 I never tidy my bedroom in the morning.
7 I seldom stay at school after classes have finished.
8 (Once or twice a week) My best friend comes round to my house (once or twice a week).

4 1 <u>am not agree</u> don't agree
2 <u>work</u> works
3 <u>stay always</u> always stay
4 <u>goes</u> go
5 <u>in the moment</u> at the moment
6 <u>go often</u> often go
7 <u>lives</u> live
8 ✔

5 1 they 2 usually 3 me 4 it 5 does 6 now
7 the 8 usually

Vocabulary ▶ p.5

1 Yes 2 uncountable 3 left, left 4 phrasal verb, informal 5 give 6 illegal 7 lent 8 on

Writing ▶ p.6

1 1 live in a small village with my parents and my younger sister
2 share a room with my sister but it's OK because we are good friends
3 free time I go to the cinema or meet my friends in the park
4 best friend is a girl called Sarah who lives in a block of flats in the next street to mine
5 want to be a doctor and work in Africa
6 favourite band is (called) Hearsay but I prefer solo singers like Robbie Williams

2 Dear Barbara,
Thanks for your letter. I really enjoyed reading it. It was really interesting to hear about you and your family.
Let me tell you about myself. There are six people in my family: mum, dad and four children. Dad's a businessman. He travels abroad a lot. He works very long hours. Mum's a dentist. I've got three brothers who are older than me and are at university in another part of the country. They just come home during the holidays.
I love living here in London. It's great and there's always something to do. We live in the suburbs but it's easy to get to the centre by train. I often go there shopping with my friends or to a concert in the evenings. My favourite hobby is dancing – I would love to be a professional dancer when I leave school. I go to special classes. Sometimes I even win prizes! Well, must stop now – I've got lots of homework to do.
Write back soon!
Yours truly,
Maria

2 Sport

Speaking ▶ p.7

1 1 paddle 2 pole 3 boxing 4 stamina 5 net
6 agile

2.1 1 both B 2 doing B 3 team A 4 go A
5 either B 6 helmet B 7 shorts A 8 game B

2.2 a) I think/I don't think b) In the first photo/In the second photo c) I'd prefer to … d) but/while

Reading ▶ p.8

1 1 join 2 wear 3 become 4 have 5 pass 6 do
2 1 at, of 2 at 3 in 4 over 5 to 6 for
3 1 tough 2 joined 3 bruises 4 fit 5 sessions
    6 face to face 7 come together 8 discouraged

Grammar ▶ p.8

1 1 Did you see 2 won 3 've/have been 4 've/have
    won 5 played 6 had 7 went on 8 were
    9 've/have never played 10 have just booked
2 1 never 2 yet 3 since 4 still 5 ever 6 for
    7 already 8 just
3 1 have you been 2 've/have been windsurfing
    3 have you won 4 Has he been able to 5 's/has
    broken 6 's/has never stopped 7 's/has just retired
    8 've/have been preparing 9 Have you had
    10 've/have read 11 've/have also started
    12 's/has been
4 1 have been swimming 2 has just won 3 scored
    4 had 5 have been waiting 6 played 7 has won
    8 have been training
5 1 have never watched 2 has been playing
    3 trained 4 have known 5 have been having
    6 haven't seen 7 have had 8 was/stayed

Vocabulary ▶ p.10

1 1 baseball 2 football 3 boxing 4 hockey
    5 tennis 6 squash
2 1 referee 2 team 3 opponent 4 win 5 wear
    6 beat 7 win 8 score
3 1 to 2 in 3 with 4 against 5 between, into
    6 off 7 over
4 1 of 2 went 3 to 4 from 5 with 6 at
    7 is 8 of

Writing ▶ p.11

1.2 A My grandparents
      1 5 8
      B The place where they live
      4 7 9
      C What I've been doing
      2 3 6
1.3 1 They've got a great sense of humour and they really
      know how to enjoy life.
      2 I've been having a wonderful time.
      3 I've met lots of people in the village and made lots
      of new friends.
      4 It's not as busy as my town but there's still plenty
      to do.
      5 My grandparents are the best in the world.
      6 On the last day, I went for a picnic with them.
      7 My grandparents' village is about 80 km away.
      8 They're not strict or old-fashioned.
      9 They've lived there all their lives and they know
      everybody.

1.4 A My grandparents are the best in the world.
    B My grandparents' village is about 80 km away.
    C I've been having a wonderful time.
1.5 My grandparents are the best in the world. They're not
    strict or old-fashioned. They've got a great sense of
    humour and they really know how to enjoy life.
    My grandparents' village is about 80 km away. They've
    lived there all their lives and they know everybody. It's
    not as busy as my town but there's still plenty to do.
    I've been having a wonderful time. I've met lots of
    people in the village and made lots of new friends.
    On the last day, I went for a picnic with them.
2 Dear James,
    I've just received your letter. Sorry I didn't write before
    but I've been so busy during the last few weeks.
    To start with, my teacher has chosen me to play in the
    school volleyball team! I can't believe it and I'm very
    excited. I've got to practise every night so I've been
    staying at school really late recently. The big match is
    next Saturday. All my family and friends are coming to
    watch – I just hope we win!
    The other thing is that I've got a new girlfriend. She
    goes to my school. I've known her for ages but not
    very well. Her name's Gloria and she's 15 years old.
    Anyway, we meet every weekend – we usually go to
    the cinema or a disco or something.
    As for my holidays, well, I haven't made any plans yet.
    Maybe we'll go to the beach like last year. I'd like to
    visit you in America but it's too expensive.
    Must go now – I'm a very busy man!
    All the best,
    Steve

3 Friends and family

Speaking ▶ p.12

1 you think **2** imagine/suppose **3** do you think
4 important thing is **5** agree (with you) **6** what … think
7 opinion **8** imagine/suppose **9** right
10 also think

Reading ▶ p.12

1.1 a) over, over b) on c) around d) above
    e) with f) up, out of g) to h) up, on
1.2 a) 7 On his way back b) 2 Some time later
    c) 1 One Friday d) 3 the e) 8 It f) 5 this
    g) 6 this incident h) 4 there
2 1 make 2 join 3 watch 4 spill 5 book 6 miss

Grammar ▶ p.13

1 1 rang 2 went 3 played, were waiting 4 met
    5 was sitting 6 swam 7 had 8 fell, broke
    9 Did you make 10 did Lisa react
2 1 had rung 2 had never gone out with 3 had
    been, met 4 got, had already left 5 had been
    playing 6 rushed, still hadn't arrived 7 had never
    been 8 had been snowing 9 got, discovered, had
    lost 10 had already bought, heard, had cancelled

3 *had* a terrible argument, *was sitting* with her friends, *asked* her to dance, She *refused,* Tony *sat* down, Amy *had put* her sunglasses, Tony realised what *he had* done, He *apologised,* Amy *was coming* out of school, she *heard* someone, which he *had bought* for her

4 1 became 2 was 3 continued 4 were 5 not
6 could 7 had 8 have

Vocabulary ▶ p.14

1.1 **male and female** cousin
male nephew, uncle, stepfather, brother-in-law, widower, son, great-grandfather, bachelor
female daughter, widow, fiancée, grandmother, aunt, niece, stepmother

1.2 1 Tom's cousin 2 Linda's brother-in-law 3 John's granddaughter 4 Hanna's fiancé 5 Paul's nephew
6 Susan's cousin 7 Robert's great-grandmother
8 George's niece

2 1 short 2 fair 3 pretty 4 serious 5 pale
6 miserable 7 stupid 8 sociable 9 moody
10 shy

3.1 1 d) 2 e) 3 f) 4 b) 5 a) 6 c)

3.2 1 short-sighted 2 left-handed 3 big-headed
4 good-looking 5 old-fashioned 6 bad-tempered

4 1 A 2 B 3 B 4 A 5 A 6 B 7 B 8 A

Writing ▶ p.16

1 **Introduction:** She's the same age as me and she lives just next door.
Para. 1: But when you get to know her, you realise she's just the opposite. She's really lively and she's got a great sense of humour.
Para. 2: I'm really keen on swimming and so is she. She loves Robbie Williams and so do I.
Para. 3: We're looking forward to going to Disneyworld and all the places we've read about.
Conclusion: As you can see, I'd really miss her if we ever moved away.

2 When I tell people that there are seven people in my family, they are very surprised because most families in my country are quite small. I love all my family, of course, but Clare, my oldest sister, is really special. Let me tell you why.
Clare's very kind and thoughtful, for a start. Last week, for example, I had to stay in bed because I was sick. She spent all her free time with me. She even lent me her mobile phone so I could ring my friends. ~~She's a bit moody sometimes but I don't mind.~~
Another reason I love Clare is because she's great fun. She's always making us laugh with her jokes and with the things she does. Every time she goes out, she brings home a funny story about something she's seen or heard. ~~She is going to be a doctor.~~
To sum up, I'd say that my sister is not just a sister but my best friend too. I'm so lucky to have her. She's the best sister in the world.

4 Time out

Speaking ▶ p.17

1.1 a) 9 b) 8 c) 1 d) 6 e) 3 f) 4 g) 2 h) 5 i) 7

2 **A Asking for suggestions** What can we …?
B Making suggestions What about …? We could …
What about (getting) …?
C Turning down suggestions No, I don't think that's a very good idea. No, that's no good
D Talking about likes and dislikes He's not very keen on He's crazy about

Reading ▶ p.17

1 1 F 2 T (it's a seaside town) 3 F (only mythical ones!) 4 F (groups only) 5 F (it was the first)
6 T 7 T 8 T

2 1 fascinating 2 latest 3 scary 4 ingenious
5 fantasy 6 unique

3 1 about 2 up 3 over 4 of 5 with 6 in
7 outside 8 in

Grammar ▶ p.18

1 1 going 2 to buy 3 to have 4 meeting 5 to take
6 living 7 buying 8 to turn down 9 taking
10 to be

2 1 b) 2 b) 3 a) 4 b) 5 a) 6 a)

3 1 practising 2 playing 3 to go 4 to spend
5 staying up 6 trying 7 to visit 8 switching
9 to eat 10 to feed

4.1 a) to tell   **4.4** a) to call
b) telling   b) calling

4.2 a) meeting   **4.5** a) to stay
b) to meet   b) staying

4.3 a) having
b) to have

5 1 that 2 to 3 would 4 ✔ 5 me 6 in
7 you 8 me 9 in 10 with

Vocabulary ▶ p.19

1 1 fascinated 2 thrilling 3 amazing 4 frightened
5 surprising 6 bored 7 amused 8 annoying

2.1 1 g) 2 c) 3 d) 4 f) 5 b) 6 h) 7 e) 8 a)

2.2 1 worry about 2 spend on 3 stare at 4 agree with 5 apologise for 6 prevent from 7 think of
8 succeed in

3 1 at 2 about 3 of 4 in 5 with 6 for
7 from 8 of 9 at 10 to

4 1 in for 2 on 3 down with 4 up 5 off
6 back

5 1 on 2 of 3 about 4 to 5 about 6 in
7 at 8 on

Writing ▶ p.21

1 1 here, them, the, their, the 2 The 3 it, here
4 it, It 5 there, It, the

2   My Home Town

The town I live in is great because *it* is only 6 kilometres from the coast. I was born *there* so I know *it* and its inhabitants very well. Let me describe *it*.

Visitors to my town are usually amazed at how old the buildings are. If you look closely, you will see that *they* date back to Medieval times. Everywhere, there are narrow little streets. In summer, *they* are full of tourists but at other times of the year *they* are very quiet.

My town is very colourful too. There are markets on most days. *They* are always very busy and are popular with the tourists who come to buy from *them*. There is a bull-fighting ring in the centre of the town. *It* isn't used for bull fights any more but a lot of concerts and festivals take place *there* every year.

Last but not least, I must mention the activities you can do here. *They* are famous all over the country. You can do all sorts of beach sports but there are lots of theatres, parks, cinemas and discos, too.

To sum up, my town is a fantastic place to be. I feel really lucky to live here/there and I never want to leave.

Progress check 1 ▶ p.22

Grammar

1   1 'm/am thinking   2 Do you know, belongs
3 are making   4 are you planning   5 look
6 don't understand, mean   7 see, don't know, lives
8 is having

2   1 I always do my homework before I go out in the evening.
2 We never go to a disco during the week.
3 I help Mum with the housework once or twice a week.
4 My brother doesn't usually come home for dinner.
5 Do you usually get up early on Saturdays?
6 My friends and I go to the cinema now and again.
7 We don't often go shopping on Sundays.
8 I go to stay with my grandparents from time to time.

3   1 landed   2 Have you been waiting   3 bought, haven't learnt   4 have tried, I've never been
5 has bought   6 I've been learning   7 has already got   8 have never heard

4   1 for   2 ago   3 since   4 ago   5 in   6 since
7 for

5   1 Angela jumped out of bed and looked out of the window.
2 The sun was shining and last night's storm had disappeared.
3 She got dressed quickly and ran downstairs.
4 The suitcases, which she had packed the night before, were by the front door.
5 She was still eating breakfast when the doorbell rang.
6 A group of her friends were standing on the doorstep.

7 'Hurry up, Angela,' they called. 'We don't want to miss the plane.'
8 She took a deep breath. She had been looking forward to this day for months. Now it had finally arrived.

6   1 ✔   2 to bite biting   3 ✔   4 to hear to hearing
5 to phone phoning   6 ✔   7 to lose losing
8 to get getting   9 ✔   10 to travel travelling

Vocabulary

7   1 of/about buying   2 from seeing   3 with working
4 for passing   5 in reaching   6 with practising
7 at losing   8 in looking after   9 of winning
10 of falling

8   1 about   2 take   3 made   4 part   5 job   6 on
7 to   8 so   9 go   10 won

9.1 1 a) thoughtful   b) different   c) cheerful
d) attractive   e) surprising
2 a) bored/boring   b) fascinated/fascinating
c) intelligent   d) interesting   e) surprising

9.2 1 exciting   2 cheerful   3 intelligent   4 bored
5 different   6 interesting   7 attractive   8 surprised

5   Ambitions

Speaking ▶ p.24

1   1 prosecutes or defends   2 repairs   3 performs
4 serves   5 carries   6 tests   7 designs   8 bakes

2   1 dedicated   2 ambitious   3 competitive
4 energetic   5 imaginative   6 logical   7 practical
8 caring

3   1 In   2 can   3 is wearing   4 is holding
5 In   6 there   7 because   8 and   9 is wearing
10 think   11 travels   12 meets   13 so   14 in

Reading ▶ p.25

1   1 waste   2 stubborn   3 compatible   4 obsessed
5 vague   6 coincidence   7 prediction   8 convinced

2   1 in   2 in   3 with   4 on   5 of   6 to

3   1 make   2 come   3 do   4 avoid   5 date   6 keep

Grammar ▶ p.25

1   1 I'll have   2 are getting   3 I'm meeting   4 I'll do
5 We're having, I'll bring

2   1 'm/am going to spend   2 'm/am going to stay
3 will probably get   4 'm/am going to study
5 will work   6 probably won't earn   7 Shall I buy

3   1 a)   2 a)   3 b)   4 a)   5 b)   6 a)

4   1 you'll arrive you arrive   2 I'm staying I'll stay
3 We'll go We're going   4 Am I helping Shall I help
5 I'm getting I'll get   6 Will you do Are you doing
7 I'll get I get   8 I'm paying I'll pay   9 It's snowing
It's going to snow   10 She's being She'll be

5   1 are going to   2 does the plane take   3 shall I give
you   4 am going to   5 is starting in   6 is going to
study

Vocabulary ▶ p.27

1   1 sheet   2 form   3 earn   4 win   5 experiment
6 experience   7 retirement   8 resignation

2   1 with, at   2 on   3 at   4 on   5 for   6 as
7 for   8 on

3   1 adj.   2 noun   3 adj.   4 adj.   5 noun   6 adj.
7 noun

4   1 immature   2 improbable   3 illegal   4 illegible
5 unimportant   6 unreliable   7 disorganised
8 disobedient   9 hopeless   10 useless

5.1   1 negative   2 positive   3 positive   4 positive
5 negative   6 negative   7 negative

5.2   1 disobedient   2 reliable   3 fearless   4 flexible
5 illogical   6 unfit   7 immature

Writing ▶ p.28

1   2, 3, 8, 10, 12, 13, 14

2   <u>ad.</u> advertisement, <u>crazy about</u> very keen on,
<u>millions of</u> a number of, <u>great</u> very well, <u>like the
back of my hand</u> very well, <u>I bet</u> I'm sure, <u>Do write
soon</u> I'm looking forward to hearing from you, <u>Best
wishes</u> Yours sincerely

6 Communication

Speaking ▶ p.29

A   I can see <u>a man</u> a woman and two young people.
The woman looks <u>a bit scared</u> excited.
The boy sitting <u>in front of</u> next to the woman is wearing
<u>a helmet</u> a baseball cap.
He's holding some <u>sandwiches</u> ice creams.
There's a woman standing <u>behind</u> in front of him.

B   The woman is <u>sitting</u> standing at the check-in desk.
He's sitting on a <u>seat</u> suitcase.
He looks <u>amused</u> bored/angry.
There's a <u>little boy</u> man/teenager sitting on the floor
playing a <u>banjo</u> guitar.
He's dressed in <u>a suit</u> jeans and a T-shirt.
There are <u>two</u> three girls watching him. They look
<u>bored</u> excited.
They look extremely <u>excited</u> bored.

Reading ▶ p.30

1   1 D   2 A   3 G   4 F   5 C   6 H   7 J   8 I
9 B   10 E

2   1 raise   2 nodded   3 shrugged   4 frowned
5 fold   6 hung

Grammar ▶ p.30

1   1 always blush, get   2 rings, tell   3 see, 'll tell
4 won't be able to, gives   5 Shake, don't agree
6 talk, will be able to   7 send, will be   8 'll have,
rains

2   1 b)   2 b)   3 b)   4 b)   5 a)   6 a)

3   1 h)   2 e)   3 f)   4 d)   5 g)   6 b)   7 a)   8 c)

4   1 you   2 a   3 and   4 had   5 play   6 my
7 were/was   8 if

Vocabulary ▶ p.31

1   1 terribly   2 fast   3 extremely   4 well
5 angrily   6 awfully

2.1   a) hardly   **2.4**   a) real
b) hard   b) really

2.2   a) quick   **2.5**   a) happily
b) quickly   b) happy

2.3   a) awfully   **2.6**   a) late
b) awful   b) lately

3   1 absolutely   2 extremely   3 absolutely
4 extremely   5 extremely   6 absolutely
7 extremely   8 absolutely

4.1   1 amaze   2 amazing   3 enjoyable   4 enjoyment
5 annoyed/annoying   6 annoyance   7 accept
8 acceptance   9 astonishing/astonished
10 astonishment   11 fluent   12 fluently
13 patiently   14 patience   15 enviously
16 envy   17 careful/careless   18 carefully/carelessly
19 happily   20 happiness   21 confidently
22 confidence   23 polite   24 politeness

4.2   1 (adverb) fluently   2 (noun) embarrassment
3 (noun) politeness   4 (noun) amazement
5 (adverb) quickly   6 (noun) annoyance
7 (adjective) confident   8 (adverb) extremely

5   1 A   2 B   3 A   4 C   5 A   6 C   7 C   8 C

Writing ▶ p.33

1   1 you ought to   2 you should   3 If I were you,
I would   4 however   5 but   6 nevertheless
7 On the other hand   8 in my opinion   9 As I see it
10 It seems to me that

2   <u>Hi</u> Dear, <u>come</u> are coming, <u>sound</u> sounds, <u>activity</u>
activities, <u>funny</u> fun, <u>great time</u> a great time, <u>way</u>
hand, <u>it's</u> is, <u>to learn</u> learning, <u>to see</u> seeing, <u>choise</u>
choice, <u>must</u> should, <u>Yours sincerely</u> Best
wishes/Regards/Love

7 Your health

Speaking ▶ p.34

1   When do you think *we should have* the barbecue?
What kind of things *should we cook*?
But *what about* the vegetarians?
Don't you think *we should do* fish instead of sausages?
What *shall we have* for dessert?

2.1   1 f)   2 e)   3 d)   4 b)   5 c)   6 a)

2.2   1 piece/slice   2 jar   3 cans   4 loaf   5 cartons
6 portion

Reading ▶ p.34

1 1 junk 2 variety 3 chew 4 brain 5 hungry
6 give up 7 protein 8 energy

2 1 because/as 2 so 3 as/because 4 but
5 However 6 Although

3 1 sensitive 2 satisfying 3 miss 4 last 5 piece
6 recommend

4 1 take 2 have 3 resist 4 pay 5 feel
6 make

Grammar ▶ p.35

1 1 … whose parents own a Chinese restaurant
2 … which sells the best food in town
3 … where I usually meet my friends
4 … who opened Planet Hollywood

2 1 what that/which 2 who that/which (or delete)
3 him (delete) 4 it (delete) 5 who's whose
6 there (delete) 7 he (delete) 8 it which

3 1 to 2 on/in 3 at/in 4 to 5 at 6 to 7 to
8 for

4 1 who was an American salesman
2 which was all the money he had
3 which were large machines
4 which used eight Multimixers at one time
5 which was owned by Dick and Mac McDonald
6 who turned out to be brothers
7 which he offered to run
8 which is now a museum and shows the history of
McDonald's

5 1 whose 2 which/that 3 you 4 him 5 about
6 about 7 of 8 to 9 which 10 that

Vocabulary ▶ p.36

1 **Countable:** loaf, piece, meal, bottle
Uncountable: money, sugar, information, energy,
cheese, advice, shopping
Both: food, fruit, time, coffee, people

2 1 many 2 few 3 any 4 little 5 some, little
6 much 7 few 8 little

3 1 a some 2 many much 3 little few
4 aren't isn't 5 ✔ 6 foods food
7 chickens chicken 8 ✔

4 1 lemon 2 apple 3 cheese, cream, butter
4 crisps 5 lettuce 6 beef, chicken 7 Coke
8 bread

5 1 hungry 2 fizzy 3 healthy 4 oily 5 tasty
6 thirsty

6 1 book 2 menu 3 course 4 portion 5 isn't
6 helpings 7 can 8 piece 9 pass 10 bill

7 1 C 2 A 3 B 4 B 5 C 6 A 7 A 8 C

Writing ▶ p.38

1 1 b) 2 a) 3 b) 4 a) 5 a) 6 a) 7 b) 8 a)

2 **Mistakes in style:**
The atmosphere is really, really fabulous!
You won't believe how good the food is!
There are loads and loads of vegetarian dishes, too.
REPORT
To: The Manager
From: Gary Brown
Subject: The Stable Restaurant
Date: 5th June 200-
Introduction
Here is my report on the new restaurant.
Situation
The Stable is situated in the city centre. It's just across
the road from the railway station so it's easy to get to.
It's open five days a week, Tuesday to Saturday from
7 p.m. to 1 a.m.
Atmosphere
The atmosphere is extremely good. There's music every
night and a live band on Fridays and Saturdays. On
summer evenings, you can sit outside in the garden.
Food
The food is delicious. The menu offers a huge variety of
meat and pasta dishes. There are plenty of vegetarian
dishes, too. Prices are extremely reasonable so young
people can easily afford to eat there.
Conclusion
To sum up, I would definitely recommend *The Stable*.
It offers delicious food, a lively atmosphere and it is
not too expensive. I think it is an ideal place for
students to go.

8 House and home

Speaking ▶ p.39

1 1 bungalow 2 outskirts 3 fence 4 cottage
5 block 6 hedge

2 1 shows 2 looks 3 can 4 is 5 is leaning
6 seems 7 has 8 isn't 9 don't have 10 has
11 is 12 would

Reading ▶ p.39

1 1 inspire 2 weird 3 piles 4 mean a lot
5 hectic 6 neat 7 reflects 8 chill out

2 1 crazy 2 proud 3 happy 4 terrible 5 keen
6 shocked

3.1 1 b) 2 d) 3 f) 4 a) 5 c) 6 e)

3.2 1 messy 2 essential 3 peaceful 4 dangerous
5 fascinated 6 safe

Grammar ▶ p.40

1 1 had 2 didn't 3 were 4 would switch 5 were
6 could 7 would let 8 was 9 had 10 were

2 1 b) 2 a) 3 a) 4 b) 5 a) 6 a) 7 b) 8 a)

3 1 would let 2 lived 3 had 4 would stop
5 were lying 6 would stop 7 would ring
8 wouldn't interrupt

4 1 I wish you would stop playing the guitar so loudly.
2 I wish we had a house like Peter's.
3 I wish the bus would come soon.
4 If only I was / were going on holiday next week.
5 I wish I could speak English more fluently.
6 If only we didn't live in the city.

5 1 would 2 were 3 ✔ 4 they 5 be 6 ✔
7 could 8 it 9 have 10 ✔

Vocabulary ▶ p.42

1 1 <u>making</u> doing 2 <u>do</u> make 3 ✔ 4 <u>making</u>
doing 5 ✔ 6 <u>make</u> do 7 ✔ 8 <u>do</u> make
9 <u>do</u> make 10 ✔

2 1 put 2 take 3 wash 4 tidy 5 put 6 put
7 pull 8 done

3 1 ceiling 2 washbasin 3 floor 4 cushions
5 wardrobe 6 shelf

4.1 1 adverb 2 adjective 3 adverb 4 noun
5 noun 6 adjective 7 adjective 8 adjective

4.2 1 immediately 2 amazed 3 luckily 4 arrival
5 illness 6 peaceful 7 noisy 8 independent

Writing ▶ p.43

1.1 1 A 2 B 3 B 4 A 5 B

1.2 1 B 2 A

2 **My favourite room**

Imagine your favourite room. Is it modern or old, tidy
or messy? The room I like most is in my *friend's* house.
My *friend's* parents are farmers. Their house is *quite*
old – about 200 years, in fact. I like all the house but
the living room *is* my favourite. This room is best in
winter because it's so warm and cosy. *There's* a big
fireplace at one end. Around it, there are lots of old
armchairs with bright covers. The chairs are so big *that*
you can curl up and sleep *in* them.
The room is really nice in summer, too. There's a door
that goes *into* the garden and when the weather *is* hot,
it's always open. There are always lots of flowers in the
room so it looks pretty and it *smells* nice as well.
The living room walls are old and the ceiling is very
low. You can often bang *your* head! There are old
photos on the walls and piles of books everywhere. This
room is never very tidy but *nobody* worries about that!
I've got lots of other friends and I visit their houses
quite often. Some of them have really nice rooms but
somehow none of them have as much character as this
room. I can't imagine anywhere nicer.

Progress check 2 ▶ p.44

Grammar

1 1 We're having, I'm going 2 I'm going to miss,
you're, get 3 I'll go 4 Are you doing, I'll just watch
5 Shall we play, is going to 6 Will you dance, will

2 1 study, 'll / will fail 2 were, would get 3 shakes,
mean 4 get 5 would ring, had 6 leave
7 had known, could have sent / knew, could send
8 switch on

3 1 who organised the barbecue were great fun
2 whose father is a well-known chef
3 I ate last night was fantastic
4 I spoke to has written a new cookbook
5 who is a celebrated TV personality, gave a cookery
demonstration last night
6 which opened last week, is open until midnight
7 I bought yesterday has gone sour
8 I ate in was empty

4 1 could 2 were 3 played / could play 4 would
turn 5 would stop 6 were

Vocabulary

5 1 way 2 healthy 3 meal 4 because 5 give
6 all 7 much 8 lots of 9 a few 10 very little

6.1 1 careful 2 careless 3 carefully 4 obedience
5 obedient 6 disobedient 7 fitness 8 unfit
9 fortunate 10 unfortunate 11 fortunately
12 successful 13 unsuccessful 14 successfully
15 patience 16 patient 17 impatient
18 probability 19 improbable 20 probably
21 hopeful 22 hopeless 23 hopefully
24 happiness 25 happy 26 happily
27 professional 28 unprofessional
29 professionally

6.2 1 patience 2 unsuccessful 3 professional
4 disobedient 5 probably 6 Fitness
7 fortunately 8 carelessly

7 1 happy 2 extremely 3 hardly 4 angrily
5 extremely 6 really 7 utterly 8 absolutely

8 1 for 2 in 3 on 4 in 5 at 6 at 7 at
8 on

9 1 tidy 2 put 3 wash 4 Put 5 take 6 put

9 Music

Speaking ▶ p.46

1.1 **People:** lead singer, audience, band, group, violinist,
orchestra
Instruments: electric guitar, drums, keyboards
Equipment: microphone, loudspeaker
Types of music: jazz, rap, salsa, pop, classical

1.2 1 disc jockey 2 musician 3 drummer
4 guitarist 5 composer 6 conductor 7 fan
8 soloist

2 1 in   2 kind   3 stage   4 young   5 because
6 probably   7 much   8 There   9 prefer
10 keen   11 whereas   12 fun

Reading ▶ p.46

1 1 d)   2 a)   3 h)   4 g)   5 e)   6 c)   7 f)   8 b)
2 1 at   2 on   3 for/at   4 in   5 by   6 onto
7 through   8 at

Grammar ▶ p.47

1 1 b)   2 a)   3 b)   4 a)   5 a)   6 a)   7 b)
2 1 if Eric Clapton is a famous guitarist
2 if Madonna comes from the USA
3 Do you know if Paul McCartney played with
The Beatles?
4 Do you know if Boyzone are still making records?
5 Do you know if Celine Dion has released a
new CD?
6 Do you know if Mick Jagger was a drummer with
The Rolling Stones?
7 Do you know if John Lennon is still alive?
8 Do you know if Eminem can play the guitar?
3 1 what time the concert starts tonight
2 who the lead singer is
3 where I can get tickets for next week's show
4 where Hearsay is playing next week
5 when the last bus leaves tonight
6 whether Martine McCutcheon is singing tonight
7 what time rehearsals start tomorrow
8 where he comes from
9 this train goes to the city centre
10 a1 have arrived yet
4 1 could   2 which   3 if   4 tell   5 to   6 was
7 will   8 know   9 let   10 from
5 1 know where I can buy
2 idea how old Eminem is
3 what time the show starts
4 whether I am right
5 know where I can get
6 if you could help
7 whether I left my wallet
8 when the box office opens

Vocabulary ▶ p.48

1 1 beat   2 tune   3 heart   4 headphones
5 lyrics   6 voice
2 1 guitarist   2 singer/soloist   3 microphone
4 drummer   5 loudspeakers   6 stage
3 1 cheered   2 clap   3 boo   4 cry   5 chant
6 tap
4 1 soundtrack   2 queue   3 lyrics   4 made
5 costumes   6 stage   7 on   8 club
5 1 turn   2 split   3 put   4 bring   5 joined   6 let
6 1 B   2 A   3 C   4 B   5 C   6 A   7 B   8 C
9 A   10 C   11 C   12 B

Writing ▶ p.50

1 1 if you could tell me what time the rock concert begins
2 tell me how to get there
3 which bands are going to play
4 what time the concert starts
5 how much the tickets cost

2.1 First, is there accommodation nearby?
Second, which bands are playing?
Finally, could you tell me if there are discounts for
students?
Also, do I need to book a long time in advance?

2.2 Dear Sir,
I've just seen your advertisement for the festival in
today's issue of 'Rock' magazine. I wonder if you
could answer a few questions.
First, I would like to know if there is any accommodation
nearby. I'm a student so I haven't got much money. I was
wondering if I could camp and I would be grateful if you
could tell me if there is a campsite.
Secondly, could you possibly tell me which bands are
playing? I'm keen on heavy rock and rap music so I
hope there will be some music like that.
Finally, could you tell me if there are discounts for
students? Also, I would like to know if I need to book
a long time in advance.
I look forward to hearing from you,
Yours faithfully,

10 Success

Speaking ▶ p.51

1 do you think   2 it isn't   3 right   4 about   5 is
6 important   7 you   8 That's   9 so   10 agree

Reading ▶ p.51

1.1 1 talent   2 theory   3 genius   4 achievement
5 environment   6 inspiration
1.2 1 bright   2 exceptionally   3 persistence
4 composing   5 claims   6 remarkable
7 neglected   8 lack the drive
2 1 went   2 achieve   3 compose   4 gave
5 have tried   6 suffered

Grammar ▶ p.52

1 1 hadn't loved, wouldn't have married   2 would have
seen, had gone   3 hadn't been so beautiful, wouldn't
have appeared   4 would have heard,
had attended   5 had passed, would have got
6 wouldn't have become, hadn't written
2 1 wouldn't have hadn't   2 became become
3 went had gone   4 won had won   5 ✔
6 wouldn't have been hadn't been
7 ✔   8 would have let had let

3 (suggested answers)
1 hadn't married you   2 hadn't forgotten my camera
3 hadn't missed the bus   4 had filled up with petrol
5 had worn a suit   6 hadn't broken my shoe

4 1 wish I had asked   2 if we had arrived   3 would
have gone to   4 I had seen/I hadn't missed
5 wouldn't have become   6 only I had seen
7 wishes he hadn't gone   8 would have had

5 1 had   2 were   3 was   4 in   5 the   6 had
7 have   8 if   9 on   10 had   11 been   12 would

Vocabulary ▶ p.53

1 1 energetic   2 inspiration   3 personal
4 Loneliness   5 influential   6 motivation
7 glamorous   8 creativity   9 successful
10 exceptional

2.1 1 b)   2 e)   3 f)   4 i)   5 c)   6 h)   7 a)   8 d)
9 g)

2.2 1 hopeless   2 unknown   3 pessimistic   4 lazy
5 clever   6 tolerant   7 courageous   8 famous

3 1 on   2 of   3 from   4 in   5 to   6 for

4 1 C   2 A   3 C   4 B   5 B   6 A   7 C   8 B   9 C
10 A   11 B   12 C

Writing ▶ p.55

1 1 at   2 in   3 at   4 in   5 at   6 afterwards   7 at
8 After

2 1 was getting   2 shouted   3 was sitting
4 saw   5 jumped   6 asked   7 started
8 found out   9 lived   10 had never spoken
11 were standing   12 happened

3 As soon as Peter read about the competition, he knew
he had to take part. It was a fancy dress competition
and it would take place the following Saturday.
At first, he didn't know what to wear. He thought
about hiring a costume but it was too expensive.
In the end, his grandmother made his costume.
He was going to be Robin Hood. When he put on the
costume he looked very handsome. His uncle, whose
hobby was archery, lent him a real bow.
Saturday came and the judging began. Peter was
nervous *at first* but he soon relaxed. He was sure he
could win but he wanted the judge to notice him.
What could he do? 'I know,' he said. He took his bow
and shot an arrow.
It was lucky the arrow was plastic. The judge was
shocked but there was no mark to show where the
arrow hit him. Peter was disqualified, of course.
In the end, the judge gave the prize to 'Cleopatra'.
Peter has never taken part in a competition again.

11 Lifestyles

Speaking ▶ p.56

1 there   2 seem   3 seems   4 get   5 seem to be
6 looks   7 looks as if   8 is punishing   9 to go
10 seems

Reading ▶ p.56

1 1 T   2 T   3 F   4 F   5 T   6 T   7 T   8 F

2.1 1 c)   2 h)   3 a)   4 g)   5 e)   6 d)   7 f)   8 b)

2.2 1 attends   2 feels   3 give   4 hunted   5 make
6 spent   7 studies   8 wears

3 1 gets in the way of   2 ancestors   3 starve
4 tribe   5 supposed to   6 up to everyone

Grammar ▶ p.57

1 1 e)   2 g)   3 h)   4 c)   5 b)   6 a)   7 d)   8 f)

2 1 would often/often used to   2 used to   3 used to
4 would often/often used to   5 used to   6 Did you
use to   7 used to   8 never used to

3 1 <u>use</u> used   2 <u>would</u> used to   3 ✔   4 <u>used</u> use
5 <u>used to read</u> was reading   6 <u>always use to break</u>
are always breaking   7 <u>used</u> use
8 <u>Were you sucking</u> Did you use to suck   9 ✔
10 <u>use to</u> usually

4 1 always telling   2 (always) used to go   3 is always
breaking   4 would play   5 usually stay at   6 used
to smoke   7 (always) used to play
8 always does

Vocabulary ▶ p.58

1 1 happier   2 the happiest   3 more comfortable
4 the most comfortable   5 faster   6 the fastest
7 harder   8 the hardest   9 better   10 the best
11 worse   12 the worst   13 more dangerous
14 the most dangerous   15 farther/further
16 the farthest/furthest   17 fatter   18 the fattest
19 more careful   20 the most careful

2 1 older   2 faster   3 healthier   4 dangerous
5 best/good   6 farther/further   7 worse   8 less
9 better   10 happier

3 1 easier   2 more sociable   3 as stressful as
4 the quietest   5 harder   6 the highest   7 slower
8 closer

4 1 most   2 ✔   3 the   4 than   5 that   6 of
7 ✔   8 the   9 ✔   10 is

Writing ▶ p.60

1.1 1 not least   2 more   3 second place   4 of all
5 conclusion

1.2 1 To start with/In the first place   2 Secondly/In the
second place   3 What's more/Furthermore
4 finally/last but not least   5 To sum up/In
conclusion

2 I think it's very important to keep customs and traditions. Let me tell you why.

In the first place/To start with, if we don't keep our different customs, all our countries will become the same. There'll be nothing to see when we go on holiday.

Secondly/In the second place, most people enjoy celebrating local customs. Carnivals and festivals are good fun. People can dress up and enjoy themselves. Without them, people won't get together so much. *What's more, Furthermore,* they'll feel isolated and not like a community.

Finally/Last but not least, I think customs remind us of our history. Without them, we'll forget what makes us a people or a country. People won't know who they are any more and won't be proud of where they come from.

To sum up/In conclusion, I think local customs and traditions play an important part in the life of a country. We should definitely keep them.

12 Inventions

Speaking ▶ p.61

1 Asking for an opinion
which do you think are the most important?
What else is important, do you think?

2 Disagreeing
Well yes, but it's not so important really.

3 Giving yourself time to think
Umm, well,

4 Making a suggestion
Let's start with

5 Interrupting
Hold on a minute!

Reading ▶ p.61

1 1 a) 2 b) 3 a) 4 a) 5 b) 6 a)

2 1 inventor 2 electricity is scarce 3 brainwave 4 manufacturer 5 employs 6 designs 7 come up with 8 set up

Grammar ▶ p.62

1 1 A new type of supersonic aeroplane is going to be built next year.
2 When was the bicycle invented?
3 Pocket-sized computers have already been invented.
4 A new satellite is going to be launched tomorrow.
5 Will a cure for cancer be found soon?
6 More research should be done on mobile phones.
7 In the future, cities may be built under the sea.
8 New inventions must be tested for safety.
9 Human cloning is not allowed in most countries.
10 The manufacturers were made to shut the factory.

2 1 Who was the television invented by?
2 Where was the first car manufactured?
3 How many mobile phones have been sold recently?
4 When will a cure be found for Aids?
5 When were the first real computers built?
6 Who was the telephone invented by?
7 Is the new road still being built?
8 Who was penicillin discovered by?

3 1 was invented 2 will be opened/is going to be opened 3 should be congratulated 4 has not been seen 5 is being tested 6 were told 7 was first manufactured 8 will be awarded/are going to be awarded

4 1 has to be cleaned 2 is going to be built 3 are included 4 wasn't allowed to manufacture 5 are being sold 6 was made to abandon 7 must not be touched by 8 has just been designed by

Vocabulary ▶ p.63

1 A lid B control panel C handle D compartment E plug F batteries G button

2 1 tin opener, open 2 video recorder, record 3 lawn mower, cut 4 fridge freezer, keep 5 screwdriver, fasten 6 mobile phone, send 7 dishwasher, wash 8 microwave oven , cook

3.1 A semi-circular B rectangular C square D triangular E round F cylindrical

3.2 1 triangular 2 rubber 3 circular 4 rectangular 5 silver

4 1 a) development b) discovery c) communication
2 a) inventive b) possible c) professional
3 a) achievable b) reliable c) collapsible d) affordable
4 a) ability b) intelligence c) technology

5.1 1 noun 2 noun 3 adjective 4 noun 5 adverb 6 adjective 7 noun 8 adjective

5.2 1 invention 2 scientists 3 intelligent 4 ability 5 actually 6 incredible 7 designer 8 technological

Writing ▶ p.65

1 1 b) 2 b) 3 a) 4 a)

2 1 Although 2 In spite of 3 However 4 In spite of 5 although 6 However

3 **To:** The Directors
From: Jane Smith
Subject: New school building
Date: May 10, 200-
Introduction
The purpose of this proposal is to recommend either a new library or a new cafeteria for the school
A library
A new library would be very nice. The library we have at the moment is not really adequate. *In spite of* the fact that the books are not very old, they are not in

very good condition. There are no computers so we can't find information on the Internet. *However*, a new library would cost a lot to build. *Although* computers are very useful, they are expensive.

A cafeteria
We really need a new cafeteria. At the moment, we have to eat lunch in the school hall. This means we have to take out tables and put them back every day. *However, although* a cafeteria would be good for some of the students, a lot go home to eat, so they don't need a cafeteria.

Conclusion
The cafeteria would be nice for the reasons I've given. However, I think a new library would benefit the majority of students, which is why I would recommend it.

Progress check 3 ▶ p.66

Grammar
1 1 They wanted to know if I was English.
  2 Could you tell me if the shop has closed?
  3 I'd like to know the way to the post office.
  4 Do you know how much it is?
  5 Could you advise us what to visit?
  6 Can you remind me what your phone number is?

2 1 hadn't missed, had left, would have caught
  2 hadn't argued, hadn't argued, wouldn't have been
  3 he hadn't bought, hadn't bought, wouldn't have had
  4 had saved, had saved, might have let
  5 had read, wouldn't have missed, had read
  6 hadn't gone, had gone, wouldn't have felt
  7 hadn't missed, would have picked, had been
  8 hadn't told, would have enjoyed, hadn't told

3 1 is always losing 2 used to spend 3 used to be
  4 were watching 5 always go 6 broke
  7 didn't use to like 8 would go/used to go

4 1 is being built round the city 2 are sold here
  3 was given a lot of money 4 has been invented
  5 isn't allowed to stay out late 6 was made to pay
  back the money 7 will be introduced by the
  government 8 was opened by Elton John

Vocabulary
5 1 what China is China is 2 the most busy
  the busiest 3 the more the most 4 the worser
  the worse 5 more cheaper cheaper 6 more noisier
  noisier 7 that than 8 the more popular the most
  popular

6 1 to 2 of 3 on 4 in 5 from 6 for 7 of
  8 of

7.1 1 encouragement 2 encouraged/encouraging
  3 hope 4 hopeful 5 forgive 6 forgiving
  7 pleasure 8 pleasant 9 determination
  10 determined 11 disappoint 12 disappointment
  13 creation/creativity 14 creative 15 inspire
  16 inspired/inspiring 17 tolerance 18 tolerant
  19 influence

7.2 1 inspired 2 equality 3 creative 4 pleasant
  5 disappointment 6 determined 7 tolerance
  8 influential

8 1 turn 2 split 3 go 4 put 5 bring
  6 switch

9 1 like 2 like 3 popular 4 live 5 music

13 Survival

Speaking ▶ p.68
1 1 g) 2 f) 3 d) 4 c) 5 b) 6 e) 7 a)
2.1 A axe B scissors C candle D spade
  E bucket F binoculars
2.2 1 e) 2 c) 3 f) 4 b) 5 a) 6 d)
3 1 don't understand 2 means 3 say 4 word
  5 mean

Reading ▶ p.69
1 1 send 2 exile 3 offence 4 pleaded 5 set
  6 commit
2 1 tough 2 outside 3 basic 4 common
  5 average 6 sleeping
3 1 in 2 off 3 with 4 by 5 on 6 about

Grammar ▶ p.69
1 1 had lost 2 had spent 3 would 4 had been
  5 had been 6 couldn't
2 1 how he felt 2 if he had broken any bones
  3 could walk 4 it was since he had eaten
  5 Jim would have to give up caving in the future
  6 if he was going to hospital
  7 when he had realised he was in trouble
  8 what advice Jim would give to other cavers
3 1 had he been he had been 2 said told
  3 if were the other members of the group safe
  if the other members of the group were safe 4 ✔
  5 had he broken he had broken 6 ✔
  7 has dug had dug 8 told said 9 had he managed
  he had managed 10 will fly would fly
4 1 would 2 had 3 we 4 told 5 be 6 us
  7 asked 8 could 9 was 10 him 11 felt
  12 much
5 1 she had lost her 2 there was anyone she needed
  3 Peter she had heard his 4 he had ever felt 5 he
  would fly her 6 if we wanted some 7 us he had
  had 8 he was happy to be

Vocabulary ▶ p.71
1 1 chop 2 dig 3 hunt 4 chase 5 lose
  6 miss
2 1 d) 2 a) 3 e) 4 f) 5 b) 6 c)
3 1 adjective 2 noun 3 verb 4 verb 5 verb
  6 noun 7 adjective 8 noun 9 adverb
  10 noun 11 adjective 12 verb 13 adjective
  14 noun 15 noun

4 1 difficulty 2 advice 3 suitable
4 Unfortunately 5 reliable 6 disappearance
7 rescuers 8 survival

Writing ▶ p.72

1 1 fantastic 2 spectacular 3 marvellous
4 dreadful 5 terrible 6 stared 7 rushed
8 terrified 9 screamed 10 grabbed

2.1 we've gone we went, were walking walked,
was starting started, can could, I've stayed
I stayed, they've sent they sent

2.2 pretty/beautiful/spectacular valley,
lovely/steep/fantastic path, a gorgeous/lovely/
wonderful day, a refreshing drink, a pleasant/an
enjoyable experience, happy/delighted/relieved

14 Animal kingdom

Speaking ▶ p.73

A Describing a picture
You can see in the picture that …

B Giving examples
For instance, …

C Adding another reason
Besides, …

D Giving reasons for your opinion
I've read that …

1 can see in the picture that 2 instance 3 Besides
4 read that

Reading ▶ p.73

1.1 A cage B wetsuit C snorkel D mask E rope
F bubbles

1.2 1 c) 2 e) 3 f) 4 d) 5 a) 6 b)

2 1 swallow 2 provoked 3 reinforce
4 undermine 5 jolted 6 struggle 7 revise

3.1 1 g) 2 f) 3 h) 4 j) 5 b) 6 a) 7 e) 8 c)
9 d) 10 i)

3.2 1 murky 2 harmless 3 graceful
4 unpredictable 5 huge

Grammar ▶ p.74

1 1 a) 2 a) 3 b) 4 b) 5 b) 6 b) 7 b) 8 a)

2 1 buying the dog a new collar 2 to look for my
hamster 3 me not to put my hand in the cage
4 to give the dog away unless someone took it for a
walk 5 not to go near the snake 6 leaving the gate
open

3 1 c) 2 e) 3 f) 4 a) 5 b) 6 d)

4 1 a 2 but 3 was 4 had 5 to 6 were
7 when 8 there 9 not 10 be 11 her 12 time

Vocabulary ▶ p.75

1 1 pleasure 2 conservation 3 strength 4 life
5 behaviour 6 patience 7 possibility 8 choice

2 1 on 2 against 3 from 4 for 5 to 6 of
7 to 8 for

3 1 uncommon 2 unfit 3 illegal 4 disloyal
5 impatient 6 unpredictable 7 unsafe
8 unsuitable 9 untrue/false 10 misunderstood

4 1 A 2 C 3 B 4 C 5 C 6 B 7 A 8 C
9 A 10 D 11 D 12 C 13 A

Writing ▶ p.77

1 1 because 2 As 3 That's why 4 so 5 As
6 so

2 1 a) 2 a) 3 b) 4 a)

3 (suggested topic sentences)
Are you thinking of buying a pet?
Imagine how friendly cats are.
Cats are incredibly easy to look after, too.
Just think how little space cats need.

15 Fashion

Speaking ▶ p.78

1 1 I wouldn't be seen dead 2 I don't mind 3 I'm
very choosy 4 I can't stand 5 I'd definitely have

2 1 scarf 2 waistcoat 3 trainers 4 skirt
5 trousers

Reading ▶ p.79

1.1 1 d) 2 f) 3 h) 4 b) 5 g) 6 c) 7 a) 8 e)

1.2 1 scare 2 distinguish 3 pursuing 4 affects
5 soothe 6 dyed 7 symbolised 8 dictates

2 1 dazzled 2 textiles 3 cosmetics 4 ripe
5 sorrow 6 rituals 7 go for 8 wealthy

3 1 dye 2 paint 3 decorate 4 clash 5 suit

4 1 under 2 into 3 between 4 In 5 with
6 within

Grammar ▶ p.80

1 1 f) 2 c) 3 e) 4 d) 5 a) 6 b)

2 1 to have my hair cut 2 to have 3 to have worn
4 to have a tooth filled 5 to have been 6 have
your hair dyed 7 is known 8 his arm tattooed

3 1 a dinner jacket made 2 had her bracelet stolen
3 my trousers altered 4 are going to have/are getting
the flowers delivered to us 5 had her photo taken by
a reporter 6 having/getting my hair dyed
7 have had my jacket dry-cleaned
8 is having/getting his arm tattooed

4 1 is expected to become 2 had my hair cut
3 is believed that 4 are considered to be 5 have
my trousers shortened 6 to have worn 7 are said to
have stolen 8 had my ears pierced 9 had her dress
designed 10 is thought to be

Vocabulary ▶ p.81

1 blouse W overalls B waistcoat B cap B
tights W trainers B dinner jacket M dress W
earrings B cardigan B scarf B brooch W

2.1 1 **opinion:** fantastic, amazing, awful, pretty
2 **size/shape:** small, tight, loose, high-heeled
3 **colour:** dark green, navy, purple, maroon
4 **pattern:** striped, checked   5 **origin:** French, Russian, Brazilian   6 **material:** satin, silk, cotton, leather, denim, linen

2.2 1 long-sleeved, green cotton shirt   2 ✔   3 fantastic, red leather trousers   4 ✔   5 long, blue silk dress
6 long, baggy linen trousers

3 1 wear   2 carry   3 get dressed   4 suit   5 fit
6 match   7 put on   8 clash   9 go with

4 1 she   2 in   3 had   4 and   5 first   6 they
7 fit   8 dressed   9 wear   10 looks   11 puts
12 into

Writing ▶ p.82

1 1 In the first place   2 However   3 On the other hand   4 In conclusion

2 Some parents are very strict with their children and make them wear certain types of clothes. I don't agree with this.

I think young people should be able to wear the clothes they want, most of the time. Young people want to look like other people in their group. They don't want to look different. If their parents choose their clothes, their friends will laugh at them.

The only problem is, some young people want to spend too much on clothes. They want designer labels. Other kids want things like studs and tattoos, which might not be a good idea. They might be sorry when they get older. So sometimes parents know better.

On the other hand, most kids are sensible. If they are allowed to choose, they won't buy stupid things. However, if they have to wear what their parents say and they look old-fashioned, they will lose confidence and this could affect their lives in a bad way.

To sum up, I would say that young people should be given lots of freedom to choose their clothes. However, in return for this, they must agree to act responsibly and not demand too much from their parents.

16 Our environment

Speaking ▶ p.83

1 do you think   2 we must   3 important   4 better
5 because   6 decided   7 need to think   8 should definitely

Reading ▶ p.83

1.1 1 f)   2 e)   3 b)   4 d)   5 a)   6 c)

1.2 1 traffic jam   2 parking space   3 bike lane(s)
4 inner city   5 public transport   6 number plate

2 1 coped   2 switch   3 fare   4 heads for
5 banned   6 lift   7 outskirts   8 pick them up

3 1 residents   2 the disabled   3 employees
4 employers   5 pedestrians   6 authorities
7 commuters

4 1 by   2 outside   3 on   4 on   5 by   6 on
7 at   8 under

Grammar ▶ p.84

1 1 computers will have become smaller and more powerful   2 doctors may have found a cure for cancer   3 self-cleaning cars will probably have been invented   4 more animals will have become extinct
5 sea levels will have risen by a few centimetres
6 people on Earth may have made contact with life on other planets   7 new planets may have been discovered   8 engineers may have built robots that can feel emotion

2 1 may be living   2 will have changed   3 may have discovered   4 will have stopped   5 will be studying
6 be learning   7 will have changed
8 will be listening

3 1 Will you be, will be having   2 will have got married   3 'll see   4 will discover   5 will still be coming   6 will you have learnt

4 1 we'll be landing   2 be lying   3 you'll pass
4 I'll be sitting   5 you'll drop   6 be learning
7 I'll be waiting   8 I'll tell

5 1 been   2 the   3 be   4 will   5 ✔   6 they
7 to   8 ✔   9 so   10 who   11 at   12 ✔

Vocabulary ▶ p.86

1.1 1 a) threaten   b) practise   c) decide   d) destroy
e) recycle   2 a) disappearance   b) information
c) safety   d) restriction   3 a) poisonous
b) destructive   c) natural   d) harmful/harmless
e) polluted/polluting   f) safe

1.2 1 extinction   2 danger   3 harmful   4 polluted
5 destroy   6 environmental   7 recycle   8 safe

2 1 keep   2 use   3 cut   4 look   5 cut   6 give

3 1 D   2 C   3 C   4 A   5 B   6 C   7 A   8 B
9 B   10 B   11 C   12 B   13 A

Writing ▶ p.87

1 1 a full description of the school, how much will the talk cost   2 **Para.2:** the time we want the talk
Para.3: equipment we have at school
Para.4: map enclosed

2 **Introduction:** Thank you very much for agreeing to come and give a talk to our school.

Para.2 missing item: I would be grateful if you could start the talk at 3 p.m. because our classes will be finished then.

Para.3 missing item: Our school is very well equipped so there's no need to bring a TV or video with you – in fact, we have three videos so you can take your pick!

Conclusion: I am enclosing the map you requested with this letter. Please let me know if you need any more information.

I look forward to seeing you soon,

Progress check 4 ▶ p.88

Grammar

1
1 he was going on holiday the next day/the day after
2 (that) they had never been camping before
3 he would ring her as soon as he could
4 (that) they had done most of their packing the night/day before
5 she didn't think our plane would leave on time
6 how much the tickets were
7 Pete if he had remembered his passport
8 if he had brought his mobile phone

2
1 that we didn't play not to play   2 ✔
3 us to go that we go   4 that I feed me to feed
5 helping me to help me   6 ✔   7 to not handle not to handle   8 letting me to let me

3
1 The castle is said to be haunted.
2 The bridge is said to have collapsed.
3 Aromatherapy is said to be very relaxing.
4 People with red hair are believed to be passionate.
5 Two men are known to have been injured in the crash.
6 It is said that many animals are endangered.

4
1 had her hair cut   2 to have the car serviced
3 had your ears pierced   4 have your eyes tested
5 had a conservatory built   6 had her wedding dress made

5
1 I'll be lying   2 Will you have got   3 I'll be using
4 Will you still be living   5 may have become
6 I'll still be learning

Vocabulary

6.1   1 f)   2 c)   3 e)   4 b)   5 d)   6 a)

6.2   1 pollute the atmosphere   2 endanger wildlife
3 made friends   4 built a house
5 wore clothes   6 carries a stick

7   1 put   2 look   3 make   4 carry   5 came/has come   6 used

8   1 from   2 with   3 to   4 at   5 from   6 of
7 for   8 on

9.1   1 pride   2 safety   3 safe   4 harmful/harmless
5 harm   6 threatening   7 threaten   8 life
9 live/lively   10 pleasure   11 please
12 dangerous   13 endanger   14 variety   15 vary

9.2   1 threatening   2 safe   3 dangerous   4 harmful
5 variety   6 life

17 Celebrations

Speaking ▶ p.90

compare and contrast these photos
say which event you'd prefer to be at
1 the people look as if they live in Russia
2 they are sitting in a big park
3 There's a stage in the distance
4 Some of the people look older
5 the people in both photos are enjoying themselves
6 different to anything I have seen before

Reading ▶ p.91

1
1 participant   2 founder   3 expert   4 slave
5 master   6 immigrant

2
1 made   2 died   3 dreamt   4 made   5 join
6 take

Grammar ▶ p.91

1
1 such   2 such a   3 so   4 such   5 such   6 so
7 so   8 such   9 so   10 such

2
1 too important for him to miss   2 too hot for them to wear   3 too expensive for Tom to buy
4 too late for me to go to the concert   5 too slow (for us) to dance to   6 too crowded for Sarah to walk along   7 too uncomfortable for them to sit on
8 too busy to watch the parade

3
1 too   2 very   3 enough   4 such   5 so   6 too
7 so   8 so

4
1 enough cheap cheap enough   2 ✔   3 for wearing to wear   4 enough warm warm enough   5 them (delete)   6 to sit to sit on   7 enough long long enough   8 ✔

5
1 for   2 a   3 them   4 enough   5 ✔   6 too
7 a   8 ✔

6
1 such a fabulous   2 tall enough to see   3 for us to sit   4 danced so much   5 so excited (that) we
6 too nervous to sit   7 old enough to buy
8 such good dancers (that)   9 too bright for us to
10 too expensive for him to

Vocabulary ▶ p.93

1
1 celebrate   2 put up   3 decorated   4 have
5 wish   6 wrap

2
1 decoration   2 decorated   3 colourful/coloured
4 fame   5 procession   6 participate
7 participation   8 celebrate   9 celebration
10 entertain   11 entertainment   12 romantic

3.1   1 d)   2 e)   3 c)   4 a)   5 b)

3.2   1 birthday present   2 firework display   3 fancy dress
4 wrapping paper   5 tourist attraction

4
1 famous   2 participants   3 decorations
4 colourful   5 celebrations   6 traditional
7 entertainment   8 procession   9 romantic
10 impossible

18 Getting around

Speaking ▶ p.95

1 **1** In **2** on **3** the word for **4** on **5** on **6** by **7** chat **8** In **9** there's **10** prefer **11** say that **12** get

Reading ▶ p.95

1 **1** hike **2** account **3** trail **4** wilderness **5** companion **6** trouble **7** doubts **8** fear **9** landscape **10** view

2.1 **1** h) **2** d) **3** g) **4** b) **5** i) **6** f) **7** j) **8** e) **9** a) **10** c)

2.2 **1** remote **2** humorous **3** talkative **4** congenial **5** rare **6** exaggerated **7** irrational **8** agreeable

3 **1** in **2** on **3** on **4** in **5** at **6** in

Grammar ▶ p.96

1 **1** needn't **2** mustn't **3** have to **4** doesn't need **5** can **6** shouldn't **7** don't need to **8** should

2 **1** shouldn't have driven/shouldn't have been driving **2** needn't have booked **3** should have told **4** Should I have paid **5** didn't need to buy **6** Did Paula need to catch **7** needn't have queued **8** shouldn't have made

3 **1** <u>don't must</u> don't have to **2** <u>ought to buy</u> ought to have bought **3** <u>needn't to buy</u> needn't buy **4** <u>didn't must get</u> didn't have to get **5** ✔ **6** <u>You ought have not</u> You ought not to have **7** <u>can to sit</u> can sit **8** ✔

4 **1** mustn't/can't swim **2** can sit here/beside me **3** shouldn't drive/have driven

5 **1** it **2** ✔ **3** have **4** to **5** the **6** it **7** be **8** ✔ **9** ever **10** ✔ **11** been **12** had **13** were **14** had **15** ✔

Vocabulary ▶ p.98

1 **People:** guide, clerk, travel agent, tourist, pedestrian, passenger, sightseer
Items to take/pack: visa, boarding card, credit card, traveller's cheques, passport, driving licence

2 **1** a bus, a car, a train, a taxi, a coach **2** a bicycle, a bus, a boat, a train, a ferry, a plane, a coach, a motorcycle **3** a car, a taxi **4** a bus, a boat, a train, a ferry, a plane, a coach **5** a bus, a boat, a train, a ferry, a plane, a coach **6** a bicycle, a motorcycle **7** a plane **8** a boat

3 **1** on **2** in **3** by **4** on **5** on **6** with **7** at **8** off

4 **1** miss **2** agency/agent's **3** hire **4** arrive **5** delay **6** land

5 **1** idea **2** for **3** arrive **4** desk **5** delay **6** off/out **7** off **8** agent's/agency **9** room **10** get **11** brochure **12** cheques **13** cards **14** made **15** about

19 The age of TV

Speaking ▶ p.100

1 **1** documentary **2** science fiction **3** chat show **4** quiz **5** cartoon **6** wildlife

2 **1** mean **2** think **3** so **4** like **5** agree **6** what **7** choose

Reading ▶ p.100

1 **1** viewer **2** audience **3** scriptwriter **4** critic **5** character **6** housewife

2 **1** broadcast **2** captured **3** create **4** concentrate **5** gossiping **6** predict **7** analyse **8** copy

3 **1** identify **2** succeeded **3** addicted **4** based **5** tune **6** find

4 **1** T **2** T **3** F **4** F **5** T **6** F

Grammar ▶ p.101

1 **1** to spend **2** watching **3** to meet **4** reading **5** Trying **6** to guess **7** Lazing **8** to operate

2 **1** computer games all the time is bad for your eyes. **2** Buying a second-hand TV was a big mistake. **3** Taking part in a TV quiz show was the most embarrassing thing he had ever done. **4** Seeing the film wasn't as good as reading the book. **5** Watching a horror film alone was really scary. **6** Making their own video was great fun.

3 **1** watching **2** to let **3** to hear **4** meeting **5** Missing **6** to hear **7** to give up **8** to operate

4 **1** silly to copy **2** careless of you to break **3** shocked to see **4** bad for you to look **5** can't help laughing **6** is no use hiring **7** impossible to hear **8** a waste of time watching **9** kind of you to introduce **10** not worth trying

Vocabulary ▶ p.102

1.1 **1** a) entertainment b) enjoyment c) belief d) variety **2** a) popularity b) amazement c) responsibility d) difficulty e) ability **3** a) scary b) fictional c) boring/bored d) cultural e) tragic

1.2 **1** scary **2** boring **3** difficulty **4** tragic **5** fictional

2 **1** hero **2** cast **3** character **4** villain **5** script **6** channel

3 **1** on **2** in **3** for **4** on **5** on **6** on

4 **1** B **2** A **3** B **4** C **5** C **6** A **7** A **8** B **9** C **10** C **11** A **12** D **13** B **14** C **15** C

20 Testing, testing

Speaking ▶ p.105

1 1 I think it depends   2 I mean, for example,   3 but on the other hand   4 No, I don't think so   5 I don't understand why   6 I think it is very important   7 I think that's right   8 What do you think   9 Yes, you're right

Reading ▶ p.105

1.1 1 g)   2 f)   3 a)   4 h)   5 c)   6 e)   7 b)   8 d)

1.2 1 watch   2 gave   3 clear   4 make   5 do   6 get

2 1 panic   2 revise   3 avoid   4 waste   5 tackle   6 ignore   7 glance   8 concentrate

3 1 out   2 up   3 up   4 over   5 on   6 with   7 off   8 in

Grammar ▶ p.106

1 1 e)   2 c)   3 f)   4 a)   5 b)   6 d)

2 1 must have passed   2 must have been fighting   3 couldn't have been concentrating   4 might have gone   5 must have been   6 might have left   7 couldn't have been going   8 might have come

3 1 can must   2 can't can't have   3 mustn't can't   4 revise be revising   5 ✔   6 must go must have gone   7 lose have lost   8 ✔   9 do have done   10 work have been working

4 1 He must have forgotten how to drive!
   2 Gwen can't have done any revision!
   3 Susan must have passed her exams!
   4 He must have phoned someone on his mobile phone to get the answers!

5 1 any   2 must   3 be   4 have   5 such   6 may/could/might   7 of   8 may/might/could   9 and   10 with   11 nothing   12 had   13 to   14 can/could/would   15 to

Vocabulary ▶ p.108

1 1 fail   2 succeed   3 take, pass   4 make   5 give   6 do   7 get   8 class   9 subject   10 course   11 topic   12 instructor   13 professor   14 teacher

2 1 off   2 off   3 up   4 up   5 out   6 out

3 1 artistic   2 musical   3 surprised   4 successful   5 psychologists   6 lazily   7 incredible   8 chemical   9 revision   10 failure

Progress check 5 ▶ p.110

Grammar

1 1 enough rich rich enough   2 for watch to watch   3 a too expensive a very expensive   4 to ride it to ride   5 such a bad such bad   6 ✔   7 so good such good   8 to look to look at   9 ✔   10 not enough friendly not friendly enough

2 1 had to   2 must   3 mustn't   4 should have   5 don't need to   6 didn't need to queue   7 ought to have asked   8 don't have to

3 1 Skiing   2 buying   3 to hear   4 Acting   5 to stare   6 to believe   7 to have to   8 laughing

4 1 He must have gone to the doctor's.   2 She can't be well. / She can't be feeling well.   3 You must have broken it!   4 He couldn't have heard you.   5 She must be a doctor.   6 He might be making an important phone call.   7 It must have been snowing all day.   8 She can't be hungry. / She can't be feeling hungry.

Vocabulary

5.1 1 c)   2 f)   3 e)   4 a)   5 b)   6 d)

5.2 1 approved a law   2 take a test   3 decorate a room   4 fight a war   5 celebrate an important event   6 raise taxes

6 1 put   2 ended   3 dress   4 set   5 make   6 work

7 1 on   2 of   3 through   4 of   5 at   6 on   7 for   8 on

8.1 1 attractive   2 attractively   3 successful   4 successfully   5 famous   6 famously   7 elegance   8 elegantly   9 goodness   10 well   11 badly   12 traditional   13 traditionally   14 fashionable   15 fashionably   16 trendy   17 trendily   18 possibility   19 possible

8.2 1 well   2 fashionable   3 famous   4 Traditionally   5 trendy   6 possibility